From
Pitt Street
to
Granby

Writing on the Wall
Toxteth Library
Windsor Street, Liverpool
L8 1XF

Published by Writing on the Wall &
Granby Four Streets Community Land Trust
© Remains with authors
Front & back cover photographs: © Liverpool Libraries,
Liverpool Record Office

Design and layout by Katrina Paterson
ISBN: 978-1-910580-28-8

0151 703 0020
info@writingonthewall.org.uk
www.writingonthewall.org.uk

Contents

Foreword

This book follows the original, *What's Your Granby Story?* that was published in May 2015 and went on to be reprinted twice, such was the demand.

This volume traces the roots of the Liverpool 8 black and minority communities from its original home around Pitt Street in the southern Liverpool docklands and its first moves towards Granby in the inter- war period.

Pitt Street was the original 'Sailortown' and we are indebted to the contribution made by the social and economic historian Mike Boyle for his contribution to this addition and his original research on the Pitt Street community by illustrating its cosmopolitan existence from interviews taken more than twenty years ago.

Mike was for many years director of the 'Go Higher' programme at Liverpool University and his research joins with ours to weld the stories from Volume One into this present book. We are also grateful to Liverpool Central Library for the photographs of Pitt Street in the inter war period.

Again however the biggest thanks are reserved for all the contributors we interviewed with their stories of how a community moved up the hill and stayed there tenaciously to live their life and to illustrate the links and extent of Liverpool's diverse maritime culture.

Madeline Henegan, Tony Wailey.

Introduction

This introduction charts the development, the stories and personal experiences of the black community in Liverpool, from its origins in Pitt Street situated in the St James ward in the classic southern docks of Liverpool 1 to Granby Street at the heart of the 'Granby Triangle' in Liverpool 8. In many ways, it is the story of the sea; it was the sea that brought people to Liverpool and the sea that was to transport them to new lands. For those that stayed, from colonies, dominions and protectorates, from imperial ports and poverty racked villages within the British Empire, new relationships and new communities were forged. This was a place which, even if it was a great maritime city, itself, 'born between slavery and famine' (De Noyer, *Liverpool, Wondrous Place,* 2002).Staying power is a feature of this historic community.

If you were poor in Liverpool you went to sea. If you were black and poor, it was even more the case. As Tony Lane notes, 'The encounter with Liverpudlians followed by enquiries about their families lead to the sea lanes of the world. So many people from this city were once crew members of merchant ships that almost everyone can find a seafaring relative' (Lane, *City by the Sea,* 1997).

The original area of significant black settlement in Liverpool, later to be known as Sailortown, was in the Pitt Street and Park Lane waterside district of St James. The growth of the parish of St James itself dated from the late 1700s through to the early 1800s. Much of the urban fabric of the area was made up of two-story Georgian houses that once were the homes of some of Liverpool's burgeoning middle class. As the city grew the area could be seen as a natural zone of transition. When the middle class became more and more economically mobile, they expanded the urban boundaries of the city, moving to newly developed suburbs and away from the increasingly laden docks.

This significant urban expansion throughout the 1700s and 1800s was by its very nature related to the development of a hugely bustling port city. In its early days, the original residents of the area of Pitt Street and the surrounding district included retired army officers, ships captains, shopkeepers, tailors, publicans and merchants.

Throughout the 18th and 19th century Liverpool had truly blossomed into a commercially vibrant international city; 'the New York of Europe', as the London Illustrated News characterised it in 1886, all of which was made possible by the comings and goings and volume of international sea traffic that crowded the river, and the number of seafarers and refugees of all descriptions that came here to live, migrate or ship out. The impact of these developments made the original inhabitants move away from the sea to the suburbs.

The origin of black settlement in Liverpool was provided by men from the African continent as they and other immigrants stepped in to occupy this vacuum. The history of British involvement with the continent of Africa spanned several centuries to the extent that by the 19th century the British possessions in the west of the continent consisted of the Gold Coast, the Gambia, Sierra Leone, and the area which in 1914 was to become Nigeria. It is the area known as Sierra Leone that is important here because it was from this region of coastal Africa that a progressive number of Liverpool's black settlers would originate and establish their presence in the city.

Further relations between Britain and the continent of Africa ensured, with the potential of the steam ship, that this coastal trade enabled easy scheduled sailings from Britain to those western regions named above. One of the pioneers of the routes for these new developments was McGregor Laird. Indeed, it was through the founding of the African Steam Ship Company and the negotiation and extent of the contract with the British Government, that Laird was able to run a regular monthly service from Britain to various points on the West African coast. It was Liverpool's shipping companies that would dominate this new brand of 'West African trade' by 1900, just as they had a forceful presence in the privateering and later dominance in the transatlantic slavery trade that followed.

English privateers had used heavily armed merchant vessels to prey on the ships of value of other nations, especially Spanish ship carrying gold and silver bullion that passed through the islands of the West Indies (Spanish Main) on their way home from the Americas to Alicante, Valencia and Barcelona. Privateers seized these ships as prizes in the name of the English Crown. These men of capital who financed their success were also heavily invested in the growing infrastructure of Liverpool. Their activities were given legitimacy within the reign of Elizabeth the First, 1585 -1603, who as the 'Sailor's Friend' made little distinction between privateering and piracy. Privateering put a structure in place for the raising of capital in the later process of transatlantic slavery, a brutal trade in which Liverpool became the most prominent player in the 1700's.

By 1897, Elder Dempster was establishing itself as a major company in the steam driven routes of this commercial enterprise to Africa. The company had taken control of almost all the lighterage facilities and the transit of cargo from ship to shore and vice versa on the West African coast. As a result it was able to control the flow and pace of this lucrative trade. It is important to point out that the barges and surf boats were the only way cargo could be handled from ship to shore in the absence of natural harbors in West Africa. The use of this African labour would form the conditions necessary for a significant black settlement in Liverpool.

In its early days, Elder Dempster ships would leave Liverpool with a full complement of European crew members. During the ship's stay at the different ports along the coast, one or more crewmen would often fall ill as a result of contracting any number of tropical diseases prevalent in that region. The choice for the captain of the ship was quite simple; he could either make the return journey 'shorthanded', or replace the stricken crew member with a West African seaman. It was from this chain of events that the germination process of black settlement in Liverpool began.

It is perhaps important at this stage to stress that the aim here is not to establish the origin of Liverpool's first black settlers - there had been black people living in Liverpool since the 1500s - but to explore and establish the contribution made by one of Liverpool's major shipping companies in the formation of a significant black presence in a particular part of the city.

In examining Elder Dempster's rise to prominence, one group of African people, the Kru, frequently appear. The Kru were involved in the building of the infrastructure of the region. It was they who played such a key role in ship work as firemen in the stokeholds of the company ships, and it was the Kru firemen who came to Liverpool.

Trading was very much a traditional and an integral way of life for them. As Diane Frost points out in *Work and Community among West African Migrant Workers in the 19th Century* (Frost, LUP, 1999) the trade was carried out in what have since become known as the Kru coastal towns. The stage was then set for the organised recruitment of African labour to work both ashore building the infrastructure of African ports facilities and on-board ship working as crew members for the Elder Dempster line.

In terms of life on board ship, the pay that West African seamen initially received was equal to that of their British counterparts. The number of Sierra Leonean seamen employed by Elder Dempster, although small in the beginning, was to increase steadily from 1870, culminating in 1902 in a full complement of Sierra Leonean firemen manning the stokehold of the ship the *SS Africa*. Throughout this thirty-year period, pay was the same as for British crew members.

After 1902, with the sailing of the *Africa* from Liverpool with a full 'down below crowd' of Freetown firemen, the situation changed. These men were paid less than their Liverpudlian shipmates who worked as deckhands and stewards. This was to form the future pattern for the terms of employment of the West African seafarer. It would herald the start of what could be described as the structural and institutional exploitation of seamen of colour.

This deliberate act to devalue the African's terms of employment would later be adopted by other shipping companies employing West Indian, East Indian and Asian and Chinese seafarers out of Liverpool. A racist culture permeated the corridors of power in the various shipping companies when it came to their attitude to these seamen. This pervaded the development of the community.

The establishment after the First World War of the National Maritime Board in 1920, legitimized such disparities with its coming together of state, ship owners and seamen's unions. The shipping companies represented on the Board who indulged in these unfair and racist practices were allowed to operate in something like an invisible floating zone, as if aboard the *Flying Dutchman,* and yet no challenge came from many of the unions, equally invisible, who were supposed to represent the seamen.

For example, trying to consolidate themselves as national institutions, The National Sailors' and Firemen's Union (NSFU) and The National Union of Ships' Stewards, Cooks, Butchers and Bakers (the two forerunners of the National Union of Seamen) could be seen to pander to the employers in terms of allowing, and indeed condoning a reduction in pay and conditions of the seamen of colour. The NSFU was too worried about fighting its own internal enemies and maintaining its aspiration to solely represent all British seamen. The Amalgamated Marine Workers Union, who challenged them and appealed for a similar rate for all seamen, were dismissed as communists and 'enemies of the British Empire'. The NSFU fought against and often broke any other representation that was not its own, including the Cooks and Stewards Union. As a result, catering staff were left without any union representation during the 'devil's decade' of the interwar period.

Clearly the union's inaction in terms of defending their black members' employment rights can be viewed as conduct that acted to legitimize racial disparities and to further reinforce and assist the intensification of racial hatred within British society. It was noted by the AMWU that lower rates of pay for disadvantaged groups did not bring with it any diminished level of racism, as trade unionists from around the world could testify.

The NSFU had come to power by the 'revolution' across the Liverpool waterfront in the 1911 General Strike. Once established by 'the forces from below', it then did everything in its power to maintain 'cordial relations' with the ship owners, particularly the powerful Liverpool Steam Ship Owners Association. It had no hesitation in playing the race card to defend itself against any 'outside' forces or those seeking democratic change within the union.

In the case of Sierra Leonean seamen, they would no longer 'sign on' to an Elder Dempster ship under British articles, which had until then been the normal procedure for West African seamen. Shipping articles were the seaman's agreed contract with the Board of Trade, which everyone had to sign when joining his ship. With the establishment of Elder Dempster's recruitment office in that part of Africa, this apparent crusade in search of economic rationalisation and sheer profit meant that those seamen and other seafarers of colour who settled in Liverpool were therefore forced to sign African Company Articles. This forced them into the vicious jaws of a poverty trap through an overriding climate of institutionalised racism in employment.

As we have noted, the area of settlement for the

West African seaman was the Pitt Street and Park Lane district of Liverpool. Elder Dempster had a specific lodging house for their seamen on Stanhope Street, close to the southern docks, and close to their ships. It is worth mentioning that West African women very rarely followed the men to Liverpool, which meant that it was predominantly single African men who settled in the city, who would therefore strike up relationships with the areas indigenous population, particularly those with Irish roots who had also swelled the inner docklands.

Because of the city's economic connection with the sea, and in turn with seamen from every country who had migrated here, either on a permanent or short-stay basis 'between ships', the area became a constant for seafarers' accommodation as well as for migrants recently arrived in the bustling port from other parts of Britain, Ireland and the West Indies. Others who found accommodation in the boarding and emigrant houses of Pitt Street and its surrounds were the almost weekly flood of Europe's huddled masses in transit on their way to the United States, Canada and Australia, as well as the constant flood of Chinese seamen.

In 1911, over 177,000 seafarers sailed from Liverpool, including those from Africa, the Caribbean, China, Scandinavia, India, Russia and the United States. This area of the docklands so close to the city truly was 'Sailortown', as Herman Melville, the author of *Moby Dick*, noted in his 1849 novel *Redburn*.

Sailortown was a rich and vibrant tapestry of peoples from all parts of the globe, who either wanted to put down permanent roots in this part of Liverpool, or who were simply passing through on its tide of constant movement.

The transition from a middle-class area to a working-class settlement provided Pitt Street and its surrounding district with a population that gave a clear reflection of what urban geographers now call a 'salad bowl' or 'melting pot', a multi –racial working-class core united by its population's relationship to the sea and dominated by dock and dock-related industries.

As with any other working-class community, self-help was very much an essential part of this urban fabric. Inter-racial marriage between seafarers from all corners of the globe, including African-Caribbean sailors, and Liverpool working class women became quite common in the district, and was uniquely cosmopolitan in a city that, by European standards, already viewed itself as something special.

This tapestry produced a number of dynamics, not least the degree of racial harmony which prevailed amongst the people of the area. 'The race or colour of a person was not something you were aware of; we all played together, we went to school together, our mums and dads were friends with each other', (Mr Joseph Boyle). This was very much the view held by those interviewed by the author. The social intercourse which existed and which played such a major part in the social fabric of the area was truly international by nature, producing a vibrant and cohesive foundation to this part of the city.

The picture then is of an urban landscape displaying all manner of life and culture; an area very much a collection of rich colours. One elderly former resident, Mrs. Margret Ann Dearden, clearly reinforces this point when she recounted her experience of living in the St James ward as a child. She spoke of how on a summer evening the air would be filled with a cacophony of musical sounds from around the world, played by an international collection of amateur virtuosos who would gather on the steps of the many seaman's lodgings and emigrant houses that made up the area's housing stock.

Such performances produced an eclectic musical mix from international sea shanties to Russian folk songs as sung by emigrants on their way to a new world. In many ways, a quite unique bond and long lasting cultural attachment was forged between the Liverpudlians who shared this dockland neighbourhood and their international visitors and guests through the enjoyment of music on long summer nights.

Another former resident, Mrs. Rachel Rigby, recalled how she would 'dance with people from all over the world' in the narrow little streets that surrounded Pitt Street. Through this process of socialization an almost unconscious class identity was forged between the emigrant, the seafarer and the area's indigenous residents a bond that transcended race, colour and creed; a consummate constituency that produced an exceptional level of inter-racial harmony that could be found in the shared experience of the wage slave and the wider daily struggle for subsistence of the 'outsider.'

These sentiments were echoed by one elderly interviewee, Mr. Larry Kee, who recalled the social interaction of the area during the interwar period, describing how the residents of Lydia Ann Street dwellings made their own entertainment. He recalled how on warm evenings the men would sit out on the steps playing their guitars, mandolins and accordions, and how people would sing and dance. 'Everyone knew everybody else', he said, and, to reinforce the point he was at pains to stress that, 'there was no racism; people intermarried and there was no religious sectarianism in the St James area'. Mr. Kee was able to talk graphically about the strong sense of community that typified the neighbourhood and, as he put it, 'no matter if you were black, white or Chinese; you were from the area and that was that'.

This was very much the view held by all those interviewed by the authors over a period of many years, and was the picture of life in the area by residents who were very proud of the level of social harmony and cohesion that for them so typified their old neighbourhood and its distinctive levels of tolerance.

For the children of the area, sport formed an important role in their lives; John Foster a former pupil of St Peters RC School in Seel Street, recalled how the school's gymnastic team was highly regarded for producing talented gymnasts, including Mike Boyle's, an editor of this book, father, Joe and his Uncle Claude. Another key leisure activity for both the adults and children of the area was swimming in Cornwallis Street Baths, which provided a quite unique experience with its own saltwater swimming pool.

It was the cholera epidemic of 1832 and the pioneering work of Kitty Wilkinson which brought about the opening of Britain's first combined public baths and wash house in Frederick Street in 1842. This formed a key focal point for the St James community. Indeed, Cornwallis Street was the only Liverpool Baths to make a profit in the 19th century, and would remain open for one hundred and sixteen years, only closing in 1967.

In terms of the economic experience of the people, Mrs. Mary Ellen Burns was asked if she witnessed any poverty growing up. Her response was emphatic: 'you didn't really notice it, we were all in the same boat and our mum's and dad's all helped each other.' Self-help was an integral and communal feature of this dockland community. In examining the role women played, and in common with many dockland communities, women went to work to help supplement and indeed raise the family budget. The work was varied by nature and included domestic service, factory work, shop-keepers and assistants, seamstresses and all the endless jobs performed on ships and in workshops near the enclosed walls of the dock.

St James's ward had its fair share of multi-denominational churches, including Roman Catholic and Church of England, and one for the area's Scandinavian population on Park Lane. All of the churches played a pivotal role in the life of the community. St Vincent de Paul's RC had its own band, which enjoyed a long period of popularity, not only in the parish but throughout the Archdiocese. The band was used as part of the celebrations on feast days and the annual church outings which were known as 'Treats', where the children of the parish were taken on annual trips to the seaside or to places such as Holywell, in North Wales.

One story, included in a booklet published in 1952 to commemorate the centenary of St Vincent de Paul (1852-1952), tells of one year the band failed to parade having been unable to 'redeem its instruments in time'. You could only deduce that the instruments had been pawned by individual members of the band to help support their individual domestic budgets; like many working-class communities this was a poor area where every penny counted.

But it is equally necessary to stress that the Pitt Street

and Park Lane district of the city was the only area that displayed such a generosity in its attitude to race. And even though Liverpool was such an energetic port, the area was the only one to witness such a significant concentration of different ethnic groupings that lived side by side in such accord.

It would also be inaccurate to describe this black community of Liverpool as forming themselves into one homogenous group. There were differences based on both cultural and ethnic grounds which acted to prevent any real form of homogeneity. West Indian and West African seamen had been coming to the city since the 1880's, and although by the 1920s they and many other foreign seafarers had settled in the Pitt Street area and lived side by side, they often had different cultural backgrounds.

However, whilst racial tolerance appears to have traditionally prevailed within the narrow streets of the southern docks, the same could not be said of the broader reaches of the city itself. The outward looking global trading links that had been instrumental in the formation of this unique community were to close over after the First World War. All of Europe, indeed the world, began to look inwards as national borders were re-constructed.

In the summer of 1919 the black community was shaken by the race riots that followed the War. Much has been locally documented on the murder of Charles Wotton, a Bermudian Seafarer whose boarding house was raided by police on Pitt Street, resulting in him being chased by both police and an angry mob to the Queens Dock where he was pelted with stones until he drowned. The level of anti-black hostility and violence was unprecedented, with organised gangs of up to

10,000 searching the city for black men and attacking them in their homes and on the street. Black boarding houses were ransacked and set alight and black men and their families were forced to move to the local Bridewell (police station) for their own protection.

It was no accident that the black seafarer was singled out as the organic cause for the stagnation of the labour market. According to popular myth abroad on the streets of Britain's port cities, it was they who were cited as the cause of such an adverse effect upon the job opportunities of the white seafarer of Liverpool and other ports. Since the turn of the century (1902) the economic strategy of paying the seamen of colour less than their English counterparts did little to quell the tide of racist feeling and tension that gripped sections of British society.

The community then faced further attack from the State, supported by the white seafarer's unions in defining 'citizenship'. In Liverpool, measures were introduced that required black workers to provide documentary proof of British nationality, a requirement that was impossible for thousands of seafarers born in British colonial Africa, the Caribbean, the Middle East, India and Malaysia. This practice of defining the 'alien', which had begun in 1905 and further refined in 1920, was subsequently incorporated into the Special Restriction (Coloured Alien Seaman) Order in 1925. Described as the 'white washing' of Britain, the order set the policy direction of the British government with regard to black workers far beyond the post-war period. This process was even more accentuated within the Chinese community after both World Wars, where stark overnight deportations took place amongst seamen without even the pretense of recourse to the law as stipulated in the Coloured Alien Seaman Order.

A climate of what could be described as institutional race hatred saw many black and Chinese seamen being forcibly returned to their original homelands. It was therefore very much a case of either return to their place of birth or face the impoverishment which would result from being categorised as an alien. The black working class of Liverpool was presented with something of a double whammy in terms of the bleak nature of their lives throughout this period.

Inter-war Liverpool was characterised by its almost total dependence upon the port, indeed 136,000 worked in port-related activities from a total population of just over 800,000. The sea and overseas trade were central to the cities existence. It was only later in the decade that the food drink and tobacco industries began to employ large numbers of people. The predominant industries were all connected with the sea in the form of shipping, dock-related industries and shipbuilding; these were also highly vulnerable to market fluctuation and the world recession.

For those who depended upon such industries, the future promised a hard and arduous struggle. Nowhere was this effect felt more strongly than in the narrow streets of the St James ward which included Pitt Street, St James Street, Park Lane, Upper Frederick Street and the surrounding streets which flanked the southern docks. These were shocks that prompted a community to look inwards, which was ironic as it was the great open sea that brought them here, where, it could be argued, the world really did live on Pitt Street.

Within this poisonous climate, the historian John Belchem reminds us that, 'by this time, the growth of the black settlement was attracting the attention of academic social scientists based at the University whose approach, however, differed little from the blend of sex, prejudice and economics favoured by other interested parties, not least Havelock Wilson's seamen's union in defence of its white members. *'On The Waterfront'* (English Heritage Conference proceedings, Liverpool 2002)

Ten years after the racial attacks, prejudice again rose to the surface with the publication of a report by Muriel Fletcher, a young researcher employed at the University. Published in 1930 as a result of the Liverpool settlement enquiry, the community's confidence was shaken by the virulence of her findings. Her survey, *Report on an Investigation into the Colour Problem in Liverpool and other Ports*, could quite clearly be seen to form the quintessential racist position held by the white establishment in terms of the way they viewed black people living in a particular area of the city.

Fletcher was particularly alarmed at the rise of Liverpool's 'mixed race' population, which the report blamed on the depressed state of the city. The report also cited the correlation between anti-social behaviour and mixed-race Liverpudlians, who it held responsible for much of the crime committed in the city. Fletcher also accused West African's of encouraging a slum landlord culture within the area. Taken literally, the report blamed much of Liverpool's social and economic problem of the period firmly on the black community; although one of the key thrusts of the report can be seen to consciously or unconsciously highlight the plight of West African seamen's families living in Liverpool, who it argued could only count on casual work and reduced wages in order to eke out a living.

Nearly thirty years after wage discrimination and

the consolidation of their recruitment policy in Sierra Leone, Elder Dempster and other shipping companies of the day could provide graphic examples of how racial discrimination could so easily establish itself root and branch within society through discriminatory practices in payment and employment for people of colour.

After 1930 though, other more positive missions were set up to help support the people of the community. In the same booklet commemorating the centenary of St Vincent de Paul an account is given of what is described as St. Benedict's 'Coloured Mission', which was formed in 1932 as a result of what the passage describes as the 'slump in the shipping industry'. The mission was located at 75 Great George Street and was run by Fr. Patrick Cullen, an African Missionary Father and one of his younger priests, both of whom were based in The African Missionary in Ullet Road, an area just above Granby in Liverpool 8.

The newly set up Mission was used to provide a regular Sunday service at 10am in the mission's chapel, which could house a congregation of up to eighty people. Other features included a recreation room like those found in any Catholic Church club and dancing at 'the Tanner Hops', which were a regular feature of the weekends.

Apart from St Benedict's, another mission for the black people living in the area was set up a year before in 1931 with sponsorship from the Church of Scotland. Pastor Daniel Ekarte opened the 'African Church Mission' in Liverpool. The main aim of the Mission was to provide a place of worship and socialisation for the black people of the area. The work of Pastor Ekarte and that of the Mission is well known among the more elderly members of Liverpool's black community. He is remembered as a community activist and black leader, whose work spanned several generations of Liverpool's black community even when that community began to disperse.

It must also be remembered that St Michael's in the City was another focal point for many of the black community in the area, with the Quarless family giving nearly one hundred years of service as vergers and wardens.

While Liverpool's employment in the interwar period was still heavily dependent upon the port, the world around it had begun to change. Gone was the free and easy atmosphere of the pre-war era where there had been no major European conflict for nearly a hundred years and trade had boomed to Britain's mercantile advantage. Shipping was in decline, and the imposition of state borders, protectionism and the growth of nationalism was prevalent everywhere.

When it arrived mid-depression, Muriel Fletcher's report brought great harm and huge resentment from the community: 'Her verdict on inter-racial marriage with negro seamen – promiscuous, ridden with sexually transmitted diseases, violent and contemptuous to their women – was damning. In most other contexts, inter-marriage has acted as a register of racial integration: in Liverpool, however, it was stigmatized and condemned as the 'social problem' (John Belchem, *On the Waterfront*, 2002)

This was a community isolated by the terms of an economic, cultural and racist ideology. Gone was the cosmopolitanism of the years before the First World War and instead a petty, national consciousness based upon protectionism, not unlike that which we are experiencing today, surrounded them.

The move 'up the hill' to Granby could be looked at in different ways of course. The bombs that fell across St James's ward all played their part, but do not explain the steady trickle away from Pitt Street in the 1920's and 1930's. The Chinese left the area *en masse* for Nelson Street and Great George Square at around the same time. The move could perhaps also be seen as one of upward mobility; a move away from the ships and the docks rather than being forced out. Granby offered more spacious housing and individual units, away from the two-story, multiple occupancy Georgian buildings and tenements of Upper Frederick and Pitt Street. Between these factors, the move to Liverpool 8 became pronounced.

This slow but steady move away from the area around the river was further accentuated by the Second World War. St James's was one of the neighborhoods that endured wave upon wave of heavy and sustained air raids in 1941, resulting in scores of residents of all races being 'bombed out' of their homes. The May blitz of 1941 was particularly devastating for the community; not only the catastrophic number of fatalities inflicted that would alter the composition of the area but also because it led to a significant period of transition and movement.

Though a small number of black families had previously moved to Upper Parliament Street, a stretch of nearly one mile up the road from the main area of settlement, it was the sustained bombing of Liverpool that proved so decisive in bringing about a significant degree of racial dispersal to the area.

The migration up the steep river streets of High Park and Upper Hill to Princes Boulevard by many members of the Pitt Street community heralded the greatest change taking place since the community itself had been formed so close to the city's southern docks in the second half of the nineteenth century.

The Granby Triangle was in the future to display the same unique multi-cultural panorama that was so much an historic feature of the narrow streets surrounding Pitt Street's dockland community. Granby was set to become Liverpool's key area of black settlement after the war.

The Granby Triangle, running from Upper Parliament Street, along Princes Avenue and Kingsley Road, with Granby Street at the centre, was to become the new historical centre of the black community in Liverpool. Years before its arrival, the area was home to artisans and shipping clerks and the merchant bourgeoisie of many countries, with waves of more affluent European immigrants, Welsh builders and office-coated workers moving in to inhabit its broad streets. More recently, in a third wave of settlement since the 1980s, Granby has become the centre of settlement of Somali and Yemeni Communities. It has always been a melting pot and an area of historic importance whose beating heart was based upon the movement of people, markets, music and the sea.

Like Pitt Street in an earlier time, Princes Park between 1870 and the end of the First World War was dominated by merchants and commerce and, like the city itself, its wealth came from the port and shipping. Many Jewish people lived here, and the great Synagogue on Princes Avenue bears witness to their name. There were more millionaires here than in any other district. The national poet of Greece, CP Cavafy, lived here as the young child of a Greek Alexandrian import and export family, and worshipped in the then recently built Orthodox Church on Berkley Street. However by the 1930's, the Cavafy's and other merchant families were leaving the area.

The streets immediately around and behind Princes Avenue, like many behind Pitt Street, contained houses which, although smaller than the mansions of the merchants, were still a good size, with basements and attic lofts, built by Welsh builders between 1870 and 1900. They serviced the shipping industry and were built for workers, artisans and the army of black-coated clerks who could walk into the city centre and to the great shipping companies.

In contrast to Pitt Street close by the river, this leased out section of Toxteth Park, was a sedate area, old-fashioned and quiet; no pubs, workshops or factories were allowed. In common with this part of Liverpool's South End, the area was safely conservative between 1918 and 1945, although Eleanor Rathbone stood as an independent Councillor from 1929 and later Liberal Member of Parliament.

After the First World War, however, the wealthy began to move out of the area, leaving behind them huge houses that could be split up into flats and rooms ripe for cheap multiple occupancy, much in the same way that had occurred in St James's around half a century before. But it was not just the merchants who left; artisans and shipping clerks also began to move out across the city in a form of lower middle-class drift. It was these streets that became the new centre and the symbolic home to the black community.

Liverpool 8 soon replaced Toxteth or Toxteth Park in the vernacular of its new citizens. The Liverpool - born black and mixed heritage population was in turn swelled by the Somali and Yemeni communities after the Second

World War. A small mosque contained within a home on Jermyn Street in the 1950's joined the huge list of other cosmopolitan and Unitarian churches that lined Princes Avenue.

The opening of the Igbo club by Nigerian seamen on Mulgrave Street in 1935 confirmed the path of this migration up from the docks. What also added to the development of Granby was the influx of West Indian skilled workers at the onset of the Second World War. Given Liverpool's historical links in terms of its long established black community, a policy was initiated that placed most of the West Indian labour into the area. The bulk of these men settled in Granby.

Under the scheme organised jointly by the Ministry of Labour and the Colonial Office, the West Indian volunteers arrived in Britain in eleven separate groups: five from Jamaica, with the rest drawn from British Honduras, the Bahamas, Barbados, British Guiana, and the Leeward and Windward Islands. These were skilled industrial workers.

It therefore became quite clear that the racist policies used against seafarers could not be allowed to stifle the recruitment of black industrial labour if Britain was to sustain production at this time of war. The overall working conditions of the 'war workers' provided a climate that was unlike that which prevailed within the merchant navy.

However at the end of the War, the scourge of unemployment was again to create tension and violent conflict between black and white workers. Once again, the official seal of approval for discrimination in employment was provided by the National Union of Seamen, which since the early 1920's was the only union recognised for 'the lower decks' at the National Maritime Board.

In 1948, with an estimated black population of 8,000, riots were again fueled by competition for jobs, though its scale nor endurance was nothing like that of 1919. Since the formation of the seaman's Union by direct mass action all along the river in Liverpool in 1911, its leadership had become increasingly anti-progressive, isolationist and driven by those supporting the British Empire League. It feared any dissent or opposition within the union; 'communists' or 'casuals' were terms bandied about, as were 'undesirables' characterised as being 'not proper seamen'.

Addressing the Union's 1948 annual conference, its Assistant General Secretary Thomas Yates made it clear that Liverpool and other British ports were to be 'no go' areas for black seafarers; 'In quite a few instances', he said, ' we have been successful in changing ships from coloured to white, and in many instances in persuading masters and engineers that white men should be carried in preference to coloured. And committees have been set up in the main ports to vet all coloured entrants to the country who claim to be seamen.' (Fryer, *Staying Power*, 1984)

The Union had used the same arguments only the year before against three white seamen in Liverpool who were leaders of the unofficial strike. Joe Harte, Pat Murphy and Barney Flynn were all jailed for nine months in opposition to union policy towards 'unestablished seamen' and their fight to make the union more democratic. Since its formation, the NUS had always played the race card to disguise dissent within its own ranks.

But in contrast to the pronouncements of the Seaman's

Union and in common with its growing black population, the Granby area started to buzz with an international flavour during this period. There were now more than sixty shops that lined Granby Street, often selling food and goods that could not be bought elsewhere. The street with its numerous general stores, ironmongers and local butchers, its international food stores, and cars beginning to line the pavement, became the international centre for the south end of the City; 'It was like a town', said Barnaciere Musa, one of its residents. The rhythm of the sea beat through its heart; the clubs, the music, the cafés, the out of hours drinking that was different to the rest of the city. It provided a place that was vibrant and exciting; desperately poor, yes, but it still danced.

There was a feel-good factor here in the two decades that followed the Second World War. Richard Whittington-Egan's book, *Liverpool Roundabout* (1957), describes the more than twenty-three clubs and 'shebeens' in the Liverpool 8 area during the 1950's. The clubs were also for eating out and to celebrate social and family occasions – the Igbo, the Yoruba, the Nigerian, the Federation, the All Nations, the Somali, Bo Gardeners, the Sierra Leone and Silver Sands, plus a variety of other smaller venues and cafes, such as Stanley House, York House and the Robert Jones youth clubs, all gave the area its identity.

Alongside its black clientele, the large concentration of night clubs were also frequented by white locals, bohemians and music lovers from across the city. In the way that skilled West Indian industrial workers had settled in the area during the war, black American servicemen, stationed at Burtonwood, near Warrington, would bring into the area R'n'B records not available in the UK. This added to the cosmopolitan atmosphere prevalent in the whole of the Liverpool 8. Granby was a great attraction to the GIs and became a welcome alternative to the staid environment of barrack life, where at one stage 18,000 airmen were based at Base Air Depot One, or BAD 1 as it was nicknamed by those who visited.

The influence of Liverpool 8 club owners also extended beyond the area and into the city centre; the Sacked Dockers' 'Casa' club on Hope Street, for example, was originally owned by a Somali Irish seaman.

British shipping boomed briefly during this period with other new immigrants to Liverpool mainly coming from seagoing communities. The new postwar immigration ensured that shipping remained at the heart of the community.

The main countries of origin of post-war arrivals were Caribbean (mainly labourers and transport workers), West African (overwhelmingly seamen), smaller numbers of Somalis and Yemenis (all seamen), Pakistanis, (boarding house keepers and seamen), Indians and Chinese (specialising in catering), who mainly settled in Liverpool 1, but some of whom came to Liverpool 8, like the Malay and Malaysian Seamen who established a club on Jermyn Street. This was Granby's heyday. Black Scousers were one of the main ingredients of Liverpool's maritime history. A longtime resident of the area sang 'I am all of Liverpool and Liverpool is all of me'. Granby Street with its busy shops portrayed an identity and a culture that had its base in the flow of goods and people. 'The constant arrival of ships made Granby glorious. Commodities from around the world could be found in the international shops that lined that street.' (Jacqueline Nassi Brown, *Dropping Anchor, Setting Sail: Geographies of Race in Black History*, 2009).

Like Pitt Street, music was the life blood of the area, and its clubs and musicians played a vital role in the development of Liverpool's most famous band. Lord Woodbine, a Trinidadian singer, songwriter, music promoter and longtime Granby resident was one of The Beatles musical mentors in their formative years. Airbrushed out of photographs and musical history, the influence of Woodbine on the 'Fab Four', is only now, nearly twenty years after his death, beginning to be recognized. Other influences were jazz guitarist, Odie Taylor and Guyanese guitar man Zancs Logie, a man who, throughout his life was very proud that he taught John Lennon some chords. The jazz pianist, Fitzroy Jimmy James, tutored Paul, and spoke highly of him as a kid 'who always wanted to pick things up. John and Paul were hanging around the Jacaranda club wanting to know anything about blues and rock.' (Curtis Watt 1996) John Lennon's first gig with The Quarrymen was off the back of a wagon in 1957 in nearby Roseberry Street within the Granby Triangle. Derry Wilkie and the Pressmen, Sugar Deen, the Valentinos and the Chants were just some of the groups of the area that had an effect upon them.

Granby was cosmopolitan in the musical tastes it gave back to the city. Eddie Amoo sang originally with the Chants and then moved with his brother to The Real Thing. They provide a thread that has run throughout the musical heritage of Liverpool 8 to the present day with artists such as Esco Williams and KOF. Curtis Watt who was the presenter of a television programme *Who Put the Beat in Mersey Beat* (1996), made two decades ago, explored the influence of black music from the USA brought over by American airmen and seafarers to the Liverpool 8 night-clubs, upon the whole Beatles and

Mersey Beat sound in general. A current exhibition *Black to the Future* (2017) by Ray Quarless and Sugar Deen amplifies the influence of musicians and the amount of clubs contained within Liverpool 8 in those years.

In the 1970s the area began to change. The closure of the southern docks that had originally brought *Sailortown* into being a hundred years earlier was a heavy blow. The decimation of Liverpool's already small industrial base added to the misfortune. Sociologist Mark Christian refers to Liverpool as being a very Americanised city and this was especially true for its young black population.

Identity versus racism became central to the youth in the 1960's and 1970's, with no jobs and the influences from across the Atlantic on their culture. When Bessie Braddock left parliament in 1970 after twenty-five years as Labour representative, the area was dealing with a new generation of youth brought up within echoes from the USA for direct political representation and a movement of Black Power, to appropriate what was taking place in the inner city areas of the United States during this period. But Liverpool 8, as Margaret Simey noted, was not a ghetto in the American sense but a mix of dual heritage families, equally disinherited, itself the legacy of Pitt Street and Sailortown.

This period saw a down-turn in the fortunes, not only of Liverpool 8 but the city as a whole. Black youth were the hardest hit by rising unemployment rates. Institutionalised racism in employment, housing and education, set against the back-drop of decades of police brutality by an overtly racist force was the experience in Liverpool 8 and generally for the UK's inner city black communities such as Brixton in London and St Paul's in Bristol. The resulting 'Toxteth Riots' brought Liverpool

8 worldwide media attention and defined public perceptions of the area for decades after.

The upsurge of anger that exploded onto the streets of Liverpool in 1981 has been well documented. Much has been made of lawlessness and destruction but a closer examination of events also reveals a high level of organisation and co-operation between all those involved. This was not a race riot, in contrast to the murderous attacks of 1919. The police were clearly the target, and more white than black people were arrested during the nine days of rioting.

With the community having been ignored, ostracised and isolated, the mainly black staff of the Methodist Centre reminded Lord Scarman, in the aftermath of the disturbances, that black residents of Liverpool 8 were British born: 'they are of mixed racial origins, so white and black families are interwoven in a complex web of loyalties and friendships and kinship networks, a mutual lack of trust and feeling of isolation and rejection in relation to the rest of the city'. (evidence submitted to Scarman's enquiry) What made the events of 1981 so angry was the absence of recognition: that the Liverpool-born black community was as Scouse as anyone in the city.

It took nearly another decade of stagnation after the 'uprising' for the whole area of the south docks to be seen as ready for 'renovation', but still the black community and Granby were not the beneficiaries. The Liverpool-born black community had to fight hard for their identity. Sociologist Paddy MacNab, who resided in Liverpool 8, stated to a council panel of enquiry into the area that, 'the sins of omission are probably more important than the sins of commission.'

In the decades that followed 1981, the regeneration proposed for Granby Street and the Granby Triangle came in fits and starts. Compulsory Purchase Orders, (CPOs) of the classic streets, that appeared so much like the brownstones of Brooklyn, dislodged many of the old resident Liverpool black community just as War had removed the inhabitants of St James and Pitt Street. Through these various phases people became sick of questionnaires, surveys and consultants - *like living in a zoo*' said one, (Vulliamy 2011) - but little changed over 25 years. Housing associations were building new estates further up Granby Street but many of the old resident community were cleared away, 'ethnically cleansed' as one resident described the process' (Ray Quarless 2011). There were still the remnants of the club culture into the latter part of the 1990's but further CPO's put an end to this.

Ed Vulliamy in the *Observer* newspaper in July 2011 commented that, 'Thirty years on from the riots, one walks up Princes Avenue. When you turn left and along Granby Street, once the spinal cord of Toxteth, you walk into what feels like a tomb… The eerie streets are all but deserted, Victorian terraced houses of good solid stock condemned, abandoned and empty for 18 years now, their windows either bricked up or covered in steel sheeting, as though to obliterate any family or human life – any memory of Christmas, love, arguments or sex the household may once have held.'

But the slender maritime thread continues. Most Liverpool families still have a relative who has been away to sea: The Somali Centre was opened in 1989 by older men who were all seamen. Their counterparts were the Yemeni seamen who had arrived in 1948. Civil war and famine have brought different waves into Granby and there is now a small and large mosque on Mulgrave Street, with Somalis and Yemenis making up the majority of the population in the wider Granby area.

They have started to change it. Lodge Lane is coming back to life slowly and even the area around the Granby Triangle shows signs of revival. But the shore life of the sea, apart from the vegetable markets, is largely missing; the bars, the nightclubs, the blues clubs and the music have all gone.

A significant development over the decade is that Liverpool's black, racial minority and cosmopolitan communities are becoming more geographically spread across the city. Many more black and Asian people now live in areas such as Smithdown Road and Kensington, the latter once considered a racist 'no go area' in a third wave of immigration to the city. Black people now have more choice about where to live within Liverpool as areas that were almost exclusively white are beginning to change as the city becomes more diverse.

A counter argument runs that this dispersal is because of the cheaper housing in the North end of the city compared to the South, as well as the fact that new migrant communities have less affinity to the Granby area than the older communities. In addition the new settlements are perhaps more about economic cost and how people are placed by the City council and the asylum services than outright choice, which again connects back to rising prices in the Liverpool 8 area.

Any development is of course to be welcomed, but there is also a feeling that an old community like Granby –with its beginnings before the Second World War - has lost its focal point, having been eroded by successive waves of failed regeneration. The insights, memories and aspirations shared within the collection of interviews in this book, from the classic districts of Pitt Street through to the Granby community, reflect the depth of feeling that local people, and even those that have moved across continents, continue to have about the area.

The experience of those who lived within the Granby Triangle recalls Henry Ford's advice that failure is the opportunity to begin again, only more intelligently. For many years Liverpool's black community has been cast in a long unrepresentative shadow across the city. The Four Corners Project, following on from the successful restoration of The Four Streets, is a vision to restore, as public enterprise, to resuscitate the dilapidated buildings on the corners of Granby and Cairns Streets and to bring back the commercial vibrancy that once characterised the area.

The monthly Granby Street market, which, like the renovated four streets, is beginning to flourish under the leadership of local community activists, is full of flowers, food and hope. These and other developments offer genuine opportunities for economic growth. It is a symbol of the tenacity, the creativity and the 'do it yourself' culture of the residents who have stayed, weathered the storm and rebuilt their own homes with the help of the Community Land Trust, which again illustrates the initiatives set up by local inhabitants.

In the determination to fight for their homes and their heritage the Granby Street Community have captured the imagination of the public, private and philanthropic sectors and in association with the architectural group *Assemble* and the winning of the Turner Prize, the art world in general The Turner Prize is the art world's Oscar in Britain but with this new-found celebrity there also comes a danger of gentrification. The beautiful houses that have been so lovingly reconstructed may be beyond the reach of those displaced inhabitants who wish to move back to the area.

Hopefully the presence of the Community Land Trust will make a difference in keeping with their ideas of social housing and social development of the area and if houses are to be sold, that they are made accessible for those on average or less than average incomes.

But for those inhabitants who fought so hard to secure a brighter future for Granby as a thriving, creative hub within the city, theirs is a testament to the formation and continuation of a community that has stretched like a thread from Pitt Street and the southern docks across nearly one hundred and fifty years of Liverpool's history as a maritime city.

Mike Boyle, Tony Wailey, Madeline Heneghan
February 2018

From
Pitt Street
to
Granby

Somebody to Look After Me

John Isaiah Quarless

My name is John Isaiah Quarless. I was born in Barbados the West Indies, that's not strictly true because my parents were planters and they say I was born in Demerara, Guyana on New Year's Day 1875. But all my family are from Barbados and I guess I am too. I was a seaman from that island, came to Liverpool and made my life here in the area around Pitt Street. I lived until I was one hundred and one years old and some say I became a pillar of the community. My story here is recounted by my grandson, Ray.

When I came over, I stayed at one of the many seaman's boarding houses in the area at that time. One of them was run by Abraham Laurence who, like myself, was also a seaman. He was from Jamaica, thirty years older than myself and had had done well. After years at sea, he had opened his own seaman's hostel on Pitt Street. He had eight daughters; Elizabeth, Lisa, Harriet, Sarah, Ann, Alice, Emma and Mary. I married Elizabeth Laurence in 1898 at St Michael's in the City, a church that was to stay close to me for the rest of my life.

I lived on and around Pitt Street, most of my seagoing life between 1890 and 1940. I was lucky to have seven children, mainly boys, who survived their childhood. I sailed on the Moore Line to the USA for many years, the *Ulstermore* and the *Verdamore* were two of their main ships in the 1920's, and the Bank Line and the City Line before them, up until the First World War. My merchant marine war medals also give my birthplace as Demerara, and that is why they cannot find my birth certificate in

1

Barbados but that did not stop the High Commissioner from coming to visit me on my hundredth birthday. My discharge books show many other trips on other ships to the States including the Dene line and Lamport and Holt ships.

I was 30 years old when the first Aliens Order was passed in 1905 to try to stem the wave of Jewish immigrants from Eastern Europe on their way to the United States. It wasn't until after the first war that I was issued with an Alien Order card myself. This was not regularly stamped until 1925.

The Alien Order card was being renewed all through the 1920s, mine ran from 1920 but was not stamped as I say until 1923 but after 1925 it became regular with the Alien Seaman's order. A seaman for more than thirty years and living in the city, I suddenly had to report to the police station at the end of each trip. You can see clearly in the book my regular attendance at the Argyll Street Bridewell where the card was stamped.

It is ironic that by 1925 when British seamen were striking and walking off ships in all parts of the empire against cut to their wages, their union was savaging them as well, via the Maritime Board which was also promoting segregation against black seamen in all the 'home' ports.

Ray, John Isaiah's grandson quotes from a book by John Belchem who comments that 'These British subjects, however, were soon to encounter the full force of British institutional racism. Various vested interest groups – shipping owners, trade union leaders, government departments and local officials – struggled to redefine British nationality so as to codify and institutionalize racial hierarchy for their own advantage.

The extent of documentary proof required by the Special Restriction (Coloured Alien Seamen) Order in1925 was an impracticable stipulation for thousands of seamen born in Africa, the Caribbean, the Middle East, India and Malaya' (Belchem, *Before The Windrush*, 2008).

I was a man who was known to take a taxi home from the distance of where my ship had berthed, whether in the north end of the city or a spit away in the Queens Dock to Pitt Street. Beside my own sea chest, the taxi would also carry sacks of coconuts and bananas for the children of the area. I always sailed above deck, first as cook in the galley and later as Chief Steward.

I finished with the sea in 1939 just before my 65th birthday after a lifetime of going away and when I passed away nearly forty years later, my death was read out in the Lodges of West Africa and Lagos in particular. I had joined the Masons in Nigeria in 1917. It was an accepted fact that Freemasonry, the Church of England and Roman Catholicism ran through black culture often as a pathway through segregation. Protection routes were always taken by West Indian, West African and indeed the Chinese community of Pitt Street.

My family began to leave the Pitt Street area for Granby during the late 1920's,well before the bombs fell over St James in the Second World War. In the same period, the Chinese community also moved from Pitt Street to the Nelson Street area where there was a huge hostel for Chinese seamen at no 10 Great George Square. That same shifting of district was evident within our own community.

My sister in law, (Ray's great Auntie) Sarah Ann, moved up to Granby on Selborne Street in the 1920's. She married Georgie Wayland, a seaman, and lived up there all her married life. George went away to sea, became a boxer, worked as a tailor and then ran The Clock pub in the Granby area. Another of my sister's in law Emma, did the same after she was married in St Michael's Church on Pitt street.

My son John, (Ray's Uncle John) who was born in 1907, married a Liverpool Irish girl, Mary, who we called 'Knobby' as there were so many Mary's among our relatives. She was one of the Clarkes who had been brought up on Lydia Ann Street. They also moved from Pitt Street to Granby. My youngest son, George,(Ray's father) who was about fourteen years younger, had to carry a box of food up to Verulam Street that we sent up there to help their family, especially when John was away at sea. These visits led to another marriage, as George later married Anne Clarke, the sister of his brother's wife. John and his wife lived on Verulam Street in the 1930's. They came back after the war to Frederick Street and later moved again to Halewood.

Most of my sons went to sea except Ray's father George who had a hearing disability. They wouldn't let him go on cargo boats, tankers or liners. Charlie relocated to Southampton when the Cunard Line stopped coming to Liverpool in the 1960's. All of them lived around Granby Street and I suppose followed a tradition that was started down here on Pitt Street of looking after others.

St Michael's in the City Church was very important in our lives. The Quarless family were involved as vergers and warden here for nearly a hundred years – and even with the Irish Catholic side of the family (the Clarkes and the Tighes, daughters of dockers,) services were quietly held at St Peter's on Seel Street away from my domain. I know Ray's mother celebrated St Patrick's day every year – but got married quietly to George in the registry office. They renewed their vows in 2001. Nearly all the Laurence daughters were married in St Michael's.

Many of the Irish side of the family lived all around the area, the Tighes on Blundell Street and Dickinson Street; the Clarkes on Upper Frederick Street, and John Joseph Clarke lived around Lydia Ann Street, Kent Street and later Kent Gardens.

Despite me tolerating this side of the family, as long as it was kept quiet, Ray was still brought up C of E and the same with his school, Church, Sunday School, Bible classes, Life Boys and Boys Brigade, and his sisters, the Girls' Friendly Society.

'We had the whole ticket,' Ray says.

George Quarless, my youngest son and Ray's father was involved with the Boys' Brigade up unto the age of 85 and followed in my footsteps as verger and warden at St Michael's. His sister Alice took her turn between 1976 and 1986. By the time of George's death in 2012 our family had made nearly a hundred years' contribution to the upkeep of the church.

Our family of seafarers gradually made the transition from Pitt Street to Granby during the 1920's and 1930's. Another of my sons, Hilary, who everyone called 'Giddy' but who called himself Frank, lived in Granby, Ernie, in Warwick Gardens and Harry, another seafarer, lived up there before the bombs fell on Pitt Street as well as John and his family on Verulam Street.

The Chinese were numbered in thousands along Pitt Street in the early part of the 20th century due to the Holt shipping company who had started the China Trade from Liverpool around the time of the Opium Wars (1835) and later through the new steam engines of the Blue Funnel Line. There was a real cosmopolitan community here.

I can give testimony to all that, living off Pitt Street and Kent Street, via the lodging houses from the time I came to Liverpool. Like Abraham Laurence my father in law, I owned my own house and rented out rooms when I was away at sea. I lived all my life around the Pitt Street area and was there in 1905, then to Kent Street. I then spent the years 1939 to-1974 on Nile Street, just next to the Liverpool University Settlement and close to the David Lewis. I came back to Upper Pitt Street in the years before I passed away.'

Alongside that cosmopolitan influence, Ray says, 'we can all trace our roots to West Africa or the West Indies but there is Ireland too, a black and green and Scouse Atlantic that the ships all brought in, it was a real cosmopolitan community.'

He notes that he has many uncles and cousins who lived in those narrow street that were variously characterised as'Sailortown' or 'Darktown'. It was a community used to defending itself because it had to. Ray's father, George, went to Liverpool Church South School, (colloquially known as St Mick's) in Cornwallis Street. He remembers him saying, 'all nationalities were in that school, we were just there, we didn't know any difference. We didn't belong to any country but were just part of our own locale in Liverpool.' .

Ray's Uncle Peter, another one of the Clarkes, a ,prize fighter and smart dresser who was a bouncer at The Nook when it was a dance hall in the 1940's and, when he wasn't boxing or going to sea, lived with their family on Kent Gardens. He used to say that besides going away to sea, all people did little bits and pieces in the area, off the back of it being on the city's doorstep.

Ray says John Isaiah looked after all the Barbadian (Bajan) nationals that passed through Liverpool –it was bigger than just a Mason thing. The way his own father in law, Abraham Laurence, looked after seaman by always running a clean hostel. Ray does remember though as a child growing up, the amount of smartly dressed men coming to the house and being introduced as, 'this is Mr Roberts, this is Mr Brown' who all came to pay homage to his grandfather. Ray is very proud of his other grandfather, John Joseph Clarke, who married a docker's daughter, Mary Catherine Tighe, from Dickinson Street whose line ran like a continuous thread throughout their family and who was the first generation Liverpool Irish to be born in the City in 1882, seven years after John Isaiah's birth in the Caribbean. John Joseph also fought in the First World War.

Ray comments, 'The communities that came before Granby have never been given the recognition they deserve . Like many families who moved up from that area, the Antige's , the Baptistes and Browns, the Eyo's, the Garnell's, Gibbons, Kelly's, McKay's, the Kenwrights from 'little Kenty, the Shudocle's, whose son Tommy came from Pitt Street and Frederick Street and who went down on the *Derbyshire* in the Sea of Japan in 1980, who all like Barney Musa, another seaman, played a huge role in establishing a black presence in the city.'

On the occasion of John Isaiah's 100th birthday in January 1975, in addition to the visit by the Barbadian High Commissioner, the *Echo* sent a reporter down to the house on Upper Pitt Street to take stock of his time in the city and to report on the celebration of his birth. Ron Jones concluded his piece by saying, 'it is not something I generally experience when I interview people for this newspaper but I felt I was in the presence of someone who would look after me.' This is what John Isaiah tried to do all of his life, to look after himself, to look after his family and to look after his community. He died 18 months later in the long hot summer of 1976. He brought a cosmopolitan existence to the city.

The World On One Street

Larry Kee

'My name's Larry Kee and I can provide you with a great tour of the Pitt Street neighbourhood; street by street by street, house by house and tell you a story about each one before the whole area got bombed in the second war. Chinese Freemasonry, the various buildings and pubs, tattoo parlours, shops, Chinese businesses and gambling houses the different gambling games including one with dominoes called Bangow, which is played with five pieces out of the Chinese set of 32 dominoes, they were all here. You could lose a lot of money at that game.

Door to door in Williams Square and Pitt Street, the place was full of people all rubbing shoulders. Two well - known police officers of the time were 'Leatherneck' a 'fighting man who would challenge and fight the local hard cases and 'Spit on the Baton' another man in black whose trademark was to spit on his truncheon before he hit you. The coach trips for the children to Barstondale in Cheshire from the 'Liddyanne' Lydia Ann Street dwellings were regular each year. The residents of those tenements made their own entertainment and people intermarried between communities.

The men would sit out on the steps playing their guitars, mandolins and accordions and people would sing and dance and everybody knew everybody else. There was no racism; people intermarried here and there was no religious sectarianism in these narrow streets.

A sense of community typified the neighbourhood no matter if you were black, white or Chinese, you were from the area and that was that. In terms of the type of jobs people did, many of the men in the neighbourhood went to sea and a lot of the women worked in the bag warehouse making sacks. It was a dirty job and the women had to be hardy to work there. On one house on Fredrick Street (he points), there was a seaman from Bombay who made 'Indian silk toffee.' All the houses of the area were not single family dwellings but more like rooming houses with different families living in them. The houses were a mixture of large two and three storey ones with cellars and attics but there were also some smaller ones that they called cottages.

In Argyll Street there was a shop called 'Copple's Cake Shop' and at five o'clock people and the kids of the area would queue up to buy a bag of broken cakes for three old pence. The shop was on the corner of Argyll Street and Duke Street. Underneath Pitt Street there were lots of tunnels that were accessible from the cellars of the houses in the other narrow streets. Folklore had it that this was the scene of murders and buried gold, especially from the houses of the old merchants, their ships and counting houses.

The Chinese Republic Progress Club at was at number 21 Pitt Street and outside it, the triangular gardens where the old women would sit, the gardens well maintained by the council. On one side of the Pitt Street dwellings in a tenement block, there was a house where a French classical guitarist lived and he would play for the children of the neighbourhood. On Lower Fredrick Street in terms of the ethnic makeup of the various families who lived there, there were families originating from every nationality- Italians, Filipino, Chinese, Indians, Irish, Africans, West Indians, Norwegians, Swedes, everyone from all around the world lived here. All the old ladies were called Aunty as a mark of respect the way they are called all over West Africa.

'There was one women called Nancy Peterower, - a very old Filiipino lady who was extremely well respected woman throughout the neighbourhood. Pitt Street provided all this as well as a certain Dutch lady from the East Indies who was known to be very rich. Before the 1930's the Norwegian members of the community lived in Great George Square and the Nook pub was where they would all drink. The tops of the tables in the pub were laid out in solid copper and remained so even when it started to turn into a Chinese seaman's pub. There was a huge hostel in Great George Square for the Chinese seamen who sailed with the Blue Funnel Line and the pub acted as a 'signing on' place.

As far as the industry of the area was concerned, as well as the bag and sack warehouses there was also a company at the top of Pitt Street and Great George Square that was called Jameson's Ships Fenders. This company manufactured all the buffers within the maritime industry and employed both men and women. As well as seafarers, many of the men of the area were employed as dockers and in dock related industries. There were ships agents everywhere and the agent of a Spanish shipping company would take payments of £5.00 placed in the discharge books by the seamen as an inducement to secure employment for the longer voyages on the company's ships. The Larrinaga shipping company was very popular in the area and the Spanish family owned company employed two agents who could always be found by Poulfords Café , near the little triangular garden.

The various pubs in the area had such fanciful names

as the Long Lobby, The Mayfair which had a vast array of pumps, The Liver, The Little One, The Lord De-Tabley where seamen still sold parrots and monkeys up to the late 1950s. A high concentration of Irish families also lived in Upper Pitt Street and intermingled with all the other races.

There was poverty on Pitt Street and I experienced it myself but it wasn't as bad as other areas of the city. There was always some money knocking about in the area because there were a large number of sailors with their pay off and someone was always getting a bonus, (he laughs). In terms of seafaring the seamen tended to sail for the same company. The southern docks and basins of the Kings, Queens and Coburg docks were well known for short sea trips such as on the Larrinaga or McAndrews Line as well as for the coastal traders.

Pitt Street and Park Lane were special places, the pubs of the area were a lot more palatial than you would find in the northern area of the city and poverty was certainly less extreme than the more industrial landscape and the court dwellings of the Scotland Road area. There was more going on in little businesses and restaurants and the difference in the type of work done by many members of the Pitt Street community.

For many people living in the area, their work was regular and not casual by nature - jobs such as carting, working on the railways, working in warehousing, in service, victuallers or chandlers of ships. Lamb's Marine Fitters was just by the Baltic Fleet. However for those who worked on the dock as dockers, life was very similar to the experience of dock workers living in the north end of the city because here was a job that was by its very nature based on the casualism of the pen system. Pitt

Street was surrounded more by small businesses than the large docks of the North End and people tended to get more regular work and more variety of work being so close to the city. Dockers came in on this as well like the Letek family.

It was partly the May Blitz of 1941 that knocked the heart out of the area but the area was changing anyway and the bombs put the lid on it. What I remember most was the smell of cooking. That same week of the Blitz was the time we saw the four bombs hit Poulfords and destroy the Gardens. The Customs House in Canning Place was hit by what they called an oil bomb. The whole city was ablaze as a result of the mass dropping of incendiary bombs. Max Simons was behind the Sailor's Home and they were always cooking. They had a sort of a cooking place there and you could smell it all over the area just like you could Coopers on Lord Street. They all got hit by the bombs. The war was when you saw the community really start to move out.'

Pitt Street and Argentina

Joseph Boyle

I am one of the old school seamen. Some would say different (laughs) I was born on Pitt Street in late 1915. I was three at the time of the 1919 race riots. I lived two doors down from where Charles Wotten was chased and subsequently murdered in the Queens Dock. My father was also a seaman – Arnold Boyle, a ships cook. He came from Barbados in the decade before the first war and married Margaret Ann Dearden who was of Irish descent and from Upper Frederick Street.

Like many other Liverpool seamen, my father Arnold went to New York for the shipping boom in the 1920's. My mother subsequently followed him to the USA. I didn't see my mother again for several years until I was a seaman myself and my ship the *Benedict* docked in New York from Para, Brazil.

I went to sea at the age of 16 in 1931 aboard the Elder Dempster ship, the *Calumet* and was placed to work with the down below crew of black stokers from Sierra Leon. I initially had a hard time of it because of being born and raised in Liverpool. The African seamen wouldn't speak to me and would tell me to go home to my 'John Bull brothers' unless I spoke with them in their own patois. I soon had to learn and I learned a lot. I have always railed against the myth of the firemen stripped to the waste on board ship as you see them in the movies: on the ships I served in, firemen were never bare-chested in the stokehold; on the contrary they wore heavy woollen shirts to soak up the perspiration. The firemen would urinate on the shovel when taking over their watch as a means of disinfecting the handle. Another man's sweat could bring infections if it got into open wounds or the calluses on our hands.

I always worked down below in the engine room: for Elder Dempster, Blue Funnel, Blue Star and the Booth Line. I spent years with each company and later became a company man with Lamport and Holt where I was promoted and sailed as a 'Donkey Man' - a Bosun of the down below crew - in charge of the ship's boilers.

Before the war I was in South Africa. I hated the atmosphere and caricature of people of colour. 'Have some peanuts' was a popular refrain. While in Durban, I was stopped by a priest as I entered a church who told me, I must sit in the segregated section of the pews, which to my mind, a practising Catholic was wrong. I replied 'why father are there two Gods, one white and one black? The situation became much worse down there after 1948.

As well as my merchant service I joined up at the outbreak of war and served in the Royal Navy. Like many Liverpool stokers I served on Q ships on the Atlantic convoys for the first three years of war and was torpedoed and sunk on the *Crispin* a Q ship designed for enticing Uboats and protecting the convoy.

I was in the lifeboat 12 hours. I was severely injured by a waving oar that smashed my groin as I clambered up the rescue nets of the Royal Navy destroyer that took myself and other survivors aboard. I spent three months in the Northern Hospital. I served on board an aircraft carrier (the *Shah*) fighting the Japanese in the Indian Ocean for three more years until peace was declared in the Far East in 1946.

Back again at sea in the merchant marine I railed against

the differential rate for black seaman and supported the 1958 International Labour Organisation (ILO) conference at Seattle for equal rates of overtime pay.

I spent over thirty years going away and moved from Pitt Street to Tagus Street off Lodge Lane during the war. I was married in 1942 at the age of 26. My wife's family, the Rigby's, were already based on the Street. I often went back down to Pitt Street to visit my Aunties Kate and Nellie who lived in Suffolk Street and finally the Pitt Street Dwellings. Following many from this city, my brother Claude emigrated to the USA in 1947 and also my Uncle Joe Dearden (my mother's brother), who left Liverpool for Canada during the war and remained there all of his life.

Considering that I was a 'down below man' all my life, I never got used to rats onboard ship and they were everywhere. I always had a phobia of rats. Maybe because one time when I lived on Pitt Street as a youngster one popped out through the many layers of wallpaper when I was in the room alone and scared me .Throughout my years at sea I always hated them.

'Self Help' was the motto of the working class community in Pitt Street which meant that one grew up with a degree of inner strength and a sense of personal independence. On my first visit to New York as a young seaman I walked from Brooklyn Docks to West 139th Street in Harlem to see my parents. It was over 30 blocks after crossing the Brooklyn Bridge, on the instructions of one of 'New York's Finest' who gave me directions. I found where they lived. My father Arnold greeted me effusively. He hid me behind the door in an attempt to surprise my mother when she came home from work. On seeing me she fainted. My father cried when he saw my callused hands. He was always a ship's cook and didn't ever want any of his sons to 'go below.'

The Rigby's were the family I married into; Edward Rigby, the father was a chief petty officer at the Boxer Uprising in China in 1911 and at the Battle of Jutland in 1917. Rachel Rigby, my mother in law was born in Henry Street, which ran parallel with Duck Street. She was the daughter of an African father and Irish mother. She also attended St Peter's school as a child. Friends of their family were the Nordstrom's who lived in Duke Terrace, off Duke Street. After they were married in 1913, Edward and Rachel Rigby settled in Tagus Street, off Lodge Lane, just before the outbreak of the First World War. While Edward Rigby was away on fighting ships, a number of the Rigby's neighbours raised a petition "to get the black woman out of Tagus Street". They did not succeed because they were supported by other neighbours. Rachel their daughter and my future wife was born and raised in Tagus Street as were her four sisters and four brothers.

One of the Nordstrom's daughters from Pitt Street, Theresa, was a friend of my future wife Rachel who was second eldest of the nine children. We were introduced to each other by Theresa while attending the Tanner Hops at St Peter's Guild Hall. Other dances we attended were at the Palais de Lo and the ones held at Saint Vinnies on Park Lane. Kitty Nordstrom, Theresa's auntie, like many other of Scandinavian descent in the area lived all her life in Duke Terrace till the houses were closed up in the 1970's.

St Peter's on Seel Street ran right through our families for marriages, weddings and christenings. Originally named St Peter's by the Sea, it opened in 1766.

Cosmopolitan, rich and poor filled its congregation with the wealthy families from Rodney Street arriving in their carriage and pairs to take their place in the designated front pews that had their names engraved upon brass plates. At the same time my mother in law, the elder Rachel Rigby remembered Chinese men with pigtails on Pitt Street in the late 19th Century. All the countries of the world, Scandinavians, Africans, Chinese seamen, West Indians, Russian's, European Jews, Armenians, Portuguese, Spaniards, Germans, Americans, Italians, seamen from Malaya and India lived there.

My mother in law's full maiden name was Rachel Carthura Boyce. She was born in 1885 in Henry Street, when Pitt Street was at its height and Liverpool was just recently entitled a city. *The London Illustrated News* called it the 'New York of Europe.' She died in 1972 at the age of 87. Her grandfather was William Boyce – who had gone from slavery in West Indies (owned by the Cumberbatch family) to a free man in Africa. Rachel Boyce's middle name of Carthura was given her in memory of an old West African mountain. Rachel's father, James Barroncloth Boyce was a m aster mariner but was never allowed to sail out of Liverpool as a ship's captain because the white crews would not take orders from a black Skipper so he always sailed as first mate. James owned his own house on Henry Street. Poverty wasn't as extensive on Pitt Street as it was in the flung up and jerry built, post Famine, North end of the city around Scotland Road. There were more layers of employment, apart from the docks, because of being on the doorstep of the city's central districts.

I spent nearly thirty years at sea until I came ashore in 1962 and worked in Fords in the boiler house like so many other seamen when factories seemed to be springing up everywhere on the new post-war estates. By then I had been around the world any number of times. After that first visit in 1939 I went to New York as often as I could, once on the Booth Boats and once in 1940 serving in the Royal Navy on board a Q ship and my mother came over to Liverpool in the late 1940s/50's and 1960's. She stayed with my Aunt Mary who lived on Dudley Road in Wavertree.

I was always interested in different places and like many seamen I was a prolific reader. I had a particular interest in languages, eventually becoming fluent in Spanish, Portuguese and German as well as the Kru patois from the early days. I was always a keen sportsman and represented St Peter's as a member of the gymnastic team, John Foster, another old seafarer who tells his story in this book, knew me there. I played football for the school and for the Navy, and deck hockey while serving on an aircraft carrier in the Indian Ocean and for the last years of the war.

I could easily have settled in Argentina like a number of others from Liverpool 8 such as Billy Masters, the great Jazz musician who became Gordon Stretton. I loved it there and sailed on the *Rubens, Romney*, and the *Raphael*, all Lamport and Holt ships that went regularly to Rosario and Buenos Aires. I loved riding and rode horses and played the football down there as well. I was a qualified referee and I did that in Argentina and for the Business and Shipping Leagues when I was back home in Liverpool.

I was always bringing stuff home, the Bolo and Gaucho horse whip from the Pampas, a small turtle and varnished flying fish from the West Indies, a penguin's skull from the Falkland Islands. All of these hopefully helped to extend our Michael's education and broaden his horizons outside of the class room.

I loved music, especially jazz, and in particular, Billy Holiday, Nat King Cole and The Ink Spots. The stepdaughter of my brother Claude, who went to New York after the second war and who married there, came to Liverpool and stayed with us in Tagus Street in the middle 1950's. Arlene was in her early 'twenties and came dressed in the latest American fashion. All the young women in Tagus Street thought she looked great. She looked like someone from the movies. Harry Belafonte was her favourite and she brought all that American popular culture of the time with her including the perfume. Her mother, Claude's wife, Betty was Jewish and a Communist. Both Claude and Betty were investigated during the McCarthy period in New York.

What always gets up so many seamen's nose is the notion that only the Cunard Yanks were the smart ones. We were all Liverpool Yanks. Liverpool always puts its best foot forward. Property owning people on Pitt or Granby Street were always aspirational for themselves and their families. Just as there are different strands of the working class, so it is within black communities, no difference in terms of different grades or status. The sea was the only employment for people of colour in Liverpool. 'Self Help' means extending the culture of your community, going beyond your own circumstances and not getting bogged down in 'victimhood' where everyone is against you and hates you, where your only self- respect is your own anger. You recognise the injustice and the straitjacket you have been born into but you work within it and against it.

Long Time in the Boat

John Foster

John Foster was a seaman who lived in various different part of the city. He was born in 1919 in Soho Street in the North End of the City then moved to Brownlow Hill. He lived on Kent Street and attended St Peter's School close to Pitt Street. When he was first married, he and his wife lived in the Granby Area and when he left the sea in the 1950's, he went to Speke and worked in the factories there until the middle 1980's. This interview was conducted just after the opening of the Museum of Liverpool Life when it was suggested by one of his nieces, Mrs Barbara Tasker of Everton, that Tony or Mike should go to talk to him about his experiences. Mrs Tasker comes from one of Liverpool's oldest black families and her grandfather was on the same ship from Barbados as John Isaiah Quarless and Arnold Boyle. Barbara notes that, 'Peter Thomas is my earliest black ancestor. He was a seaman in Bermuda during slavery. His son, Joseph Henry Thomas, my great grandfather was also a seaman. He came to Liverpool and married Grace Hamilton, a Scottish woman in 1861'. This interview, facilitated by Barbara took place in the late summer of 1993.

'I've lived my life and seen my kids grow up and we've enjoyed our time in Speke, I've made some good friends here. I was 19 years old when I first went to sea and my first trip to sea was on a ship called the *Godfrey B Holt*. I made two trips with the Holt Line on that one. I then went on to sail for the Larrinaga shipping company, where I knew a number of the crew, many of whom came from the Pitt Street area and sailed to various ports in South America. When I came home in 1939, I was only just back when the war broke out. I was 20 years old on September 3rd, the day war was declared.

On my next trip I was involved in a sinking; a ship sailing out of Salford called the *Manchester Regiment* and owned by Furness Withy. The ship was hit on December 4th 1939 by a ship named the *Europa* which was owned by P&O line. The collision sunk the *Manchester Regiment*. The surviving members of the crew including myself were picked up and taken to Canada. I then came home on a Canadian Pacific ship, the *Duchess of Richmond*, at the end December 1939. The next time I went to sea was in January 1940, the ship was called the *Barndale* and she went on fire off the west coast of Africa. John's wife laughs, 'You were a bit of a Jonah weren't you', she says.

I joined a ship called the *Baltarner* owned by the Baltic Seam Ship Company, their ships would run round the Baltic to ports in Norway and Sweden and the rest of Scandinavia. Nice short trips but we never left Liverpool even though I was on the ship for six weeks. At the time (1941) the dockers were on strike and the authorities brought the army in to load the ship. As a result of that course of action, the dockers picketed the dock gate resulting in the seamen refusing to board the vessel which meant some seamen being laid-off and others who had to stay on the ship, including me, having to remain there.

I rejoined the Larrinaga Line that was based in the Queens Dock. I sailed on a ship called the *Richard*, sailing down to South America with a cargo of coal and she brought grain back from Argentina, a familiar trading route from Liverpool. The make-up of the crews on Larrinaga ships were really what you would call 'international', normally with an English Captain, the Chief Mate would be Spanish, the Third Mate would be a Scot, the Chief Engineer also a Scot, the Second Engineer would be Greek and the various sailors and firemen would be made up various different nationalities: British, West Indian, West African's, Arab's. The Chief Steward would always be Spanish, I learned to speak Spanish as a result of sailing with that line.

The Larrinaga line was the only shipping company to my knowledge to carry such a multinational crew that was reflected in the Pitt Street area. On the Elder Dempster, the crew were made up of British officers and the crew on deck were also British seamen while down below in the stoke-hole all the firemen were West African. Another company, John Holt, also crewed their engine rooms with black seafarers but I don't know from exactly where or what nationality they were. Blue Funnel were all Chinese down below.

I have been asked many times how I would describe myself, for example, as a 'black seaman', a Liverpool seaman,' 'a coloured Liverpool seaman,' an international black Liverpool seaman'? When I first went to sea with blokes I was at school with, they were all colours. We were labelled with a name that I have always strongly disagreed with, that of 'half-caste'. For me and my mixed race school friends we suffered a lot of stick from the black side and the white side because we were half black, half white.

We, the other mixed race crew and black seamen experienced this in a more extreme form of racism in the ports of the southern United States. I would know white crew members that I had gone to school with and that they would invite me to go ashore with them. However, once they ordered a round of drinks, the barman would pull only three beers instead of four because he would refuse to serve me! As a result my white friends would walk out of the bar in support. But it brought trouble.

Because I was socialising with my old school friends I would also find myself in trouble with African crew members and accused by the African seamen of not wanting to mix with them, the black crew members. As a result of the prejudice shown from both white southerners in the US and South Africa together with the treatment from other crew members on board ship, I would 'work the head' by advising my white friends to go ashore without me once they arrived at a port in the southern states or South Africa.

I would then go ashore with the black seamen and drink in what they used to call the 'Indian bar' or more popularly known as, 'The Black Bar'. The African seamen were only allowed in what was called 'Kaffir Bars', if you were a black seafarer from Britain you could drink in the 'Indian Bar' but you had to enter through the back door. It was all crazy. The means of transport in South African ports was by tram. Blacks however could only travel on six seats at the back and if these were already taken, other black people were not allowed aboard. At rush hour they would throw the black people off the trams and place white covers over the seats and reallocate the seat to whites. It was like the southern United States where you could only travel at the back of the trolley-buses and at the driver's concession or say so. In the southern states things were just the same or probably worse after the war.

In 1942 I joined a ship called *The Empire Cloth*, a newly built ship just off the yards on the Tyne. The boat sailed for the United States to pick up a cargo. From the time the ship set sail, to the time she was sunk only three weeks later, she never even got to carry a cargo! The ship went down. It was my first experience of being torpedoed, somewhere in the Atlantic, by a ship on her maiden voyage to the United States. Myself and other members of the crew were picked up after thirty six hours in the life boats by a Canadian Corvette. They took us to St John's, Newfoundland and I was put in a hospital there. We were then taken to Halifax, Nova Scotia, by submarine and we then travelled on to Quebec. I stayed there for four weeks before I worked my passage back to Liverpool on a Canadian built ship.

My second experience of being torpedoed was at 4am in the morning; I spent fourteen days in a life boat in the Atlantic and I was scared. The problem was that there were too many crew for the available lifeboat and some of the time we had to take turns in the water. We were eventually picked up by a neutral Swedish ship and taken to Baltimore. We came home on a ship called the *Sand Banker*, which was a ship quickly built in the thousands by the Americans. They called them 'Liberty boats.' Because of the volume of the Atlantic convoys many seamen from Liverpool spent a great deal of time on Canadian ships. British crews were always being sent over to what was called the 'Montreal Pool'. After three weeks on that, I was sent to either Baltimore or Norfolk Newport News, Virginia and then sailed to Calcutta via the Cape on another Canadian ship.

(Editors' note) John featured in a BBC *Timewatch* television programme some three weeks after this interview in 1993. His comment was that 'the life jackets all had whistles on them and that over the hours through the night, the most terrible sounds were the whistles going off as men's heads fell forward in the water and they died of hypothermia.' It provided a dramatic silence to the programme's commentary.

I sailed out regularly with friends. I would join a ship and coincidentally there would be men I had gone to school at Saint Peter's or with men I had sailed with before. There was always someone you knew, and this was true of both the North and South ends of the city.

After the war I went back to sea sailing on Harrison boats. They were based in the North end then, in the Canada Dock. It had caused a great deal of trouble when the company had moved from the South end in the 1930's. The best experience of going away was seeing the world. Although the work was hard, going away to sea was a cheap way to go around and see how different parts of the world lived.

Up to twenty years ago, Liverpool was a major sea port with all the different nationalities coming to here on ships from different parts of the world, Greece, America... every kind of ship in the world came to Liverpool. It's always been what I would call an international seaport, which goes to prove that although it does not have what you would call a huge ethnic minority population there are a lot different ones... Filipino, Chinese, Arab, Scandinavian , Liverpool born black. They might be only in small in number because they were seamen who married English women, but their influence goes much wider. The bulk of them lived in and around Pitt Street before the population moved up to Granby.

There were lots of dance halls that me and my wife and my wife's sister would visit when we were courting. There was a dance hall in Park Lane owned by a black man named Gilbert and the dance hall was called after him. We also went to another place called Walnut Street Dance just off Mount Pleasant. The dances were attended by both black and white patrons and relationships would spring up between them at the dances.

I experienced some forms of discrimination in the city. I remember that at one time in the South end of the city there was a dance hall called the Rialto and the coloured people were barred from going in there. They could go to the pictures but they could not go to the dances held upstairs. There were pubs in the South End of the city where a black person could go in the bar for a drink but they could not go in the parlour. Sadie's was one of them and the Mercury at the corner of Berkeley Street and Stanhope Street was another.

The same did not apply to the pubs in the North end of the city. There was no colour- bar in the pubs of the North end. I've been in pubs throughout the North end of the city and have not experienced any form of colour-bar in any of them. The only colour-bar for me was in the South end where the coloured people lived.

Boxing Clever

John Quarless

'I am one of the Clarkes, descended from the Tighes and John Joseph (Jack) Clarke , Liverpool Irish as well as Irish as well as being a Quarless. Me Nin and my mother were the Clarkes. They all came from around the Park Lane area, Grenville, Greatham, Frederick, Cornwallis and Pitt Street. Church was always at St Michaels, the dockside Cathedral.'

'I was born in Cornwallis Street in 1933 .Our house was destroyed during the Blitz. We went down to the shelter one night and when we emerged there was nothing but a pile of rubble where our house had been except that my mother's wardrobe stood vertical amongst it on a heap. (You could see fire stretching all the way down from Frederick Street to the Customs House). Before they were bombed out of Pitt Street, the kids down there used to swap scraps of shrapnel as if it was treasure. They'd boil it up and make soldiers and planes out it.

Me and my brother were evacuated to Bangor in North Wales. When we returned from Wales it was to Verulam Street off Upper Parliament Street, where other parts of the family had moved from Pitt Street since the 1920's. I attended Granby Street School. Granby was a very Jewish area then. I remember one old lady in the shadow of war with a huge picture of Stalin on her parlour wall. 'He's a good fellow that, she'd tell everyone.' Lots of families were moving up North Hill Street and High Park Street.'

'Previously we had very rarely gone past Parliament Street. Park Lane was the border line. Cleveland square was Chinatown. For us, Upper Stanhope Street with the

28

Elder Dempster boats and Seaman's hostel was the black area. The Jungle they called it.'

'I lived in Granby for a couple of years. That was in the mid 1940's. I came home from being an evacuee in 1943. I finished school in 1947 and went to Walton Tech until 1949. I've worked all my life in the electrical building trades and travelled the country in that trade with my first wife and our children for nearly thirty years. I worked in health and safety across the water and on other major projects around Britain including Sellafield.'

'I left one job after a good period of time when I had initially been refused the work. I was always up to speed with developments in my trade. I took great pleasure in the supervisor's expression when I was leaving and said, 'not bad for a black feller eh !!'

'Pitt Street was not only black and Chinese but full of Scandinavians up unto the 1940's. Our upstairs neighbours were Scandinavian and we'd go to parties in each other's flats. All the Clarkes, Tony, Peter, Owen, Marie, Richie, Jimmy and Billy, were my Liverpool Irish cousins. Owen Clarke was their dad. Uncle Peter, his brother, was a prize fighter and a seaman. I boxed myself when I was in the Army. I told our Noel,(a second cousin and British Heavyweight boxer who had fought in European Championship fights and was a favourite at the Liverpool Stadium for the attacking manner in which he fought) "that it was all right knocking them down but what about when you go down you've got to get up". I wanted him to work more on his defence but he wouldn't listen'

'My dad was a seaman but between ships he would work on the docks. Even when he came back home covered in dust he was a very smart man. Even today,

I love to watch the Magpies play in the garden, they remind me of my Da. He was very smart and he always got about. The smartest man I knew after my father was Sugar Ray Robinson. He was very tall for a middle weight but what great poise. All my uncles were Seafarers except Uncle George who married my mother's sister.

'By the 1960's Pitt Street, Kent street and Windsor street were all images of each other like the merging of Liverpool 1 into Liverpool 8. Some people might think of it as a melting pot but to us it was just normal. Seagoing was the same, you got work with all sorts of people and wherever you could.'

'The back of Jamaica Street was all sailor's quarters and lodging houses. Park Lane was always the dividing line between the two communities. Five of John Isiah's sons, Charles, Harry, Ernie, Giddy and John were all seamen and sailed with the Cunard, Lamport and Holt and Larrinaga lines. Two of them lived in Liverpool 1 and another lived in Granby, Ernie went to Anfield and Charlie moved to Southampton with the Cunard. Auntie Eliza had a daughter and stayed on Verulam street in Granby after they moved from Cornwallis Street in Liverpool 1'

'Granby took over from Liverpool 1 (Pitt Street) as the centre for the South end. Another auntie, Sarah Ann (Seran) moved from Kent Street to Granby when she married George Wayland, George had been a seaman but then worked on the docks most of his life. Their son Georgie was a tailor and then managed The Clock pub. A big strong man, he was also a boxer who sparred with his friend Carl Spears.'

'The sea and the docks and maritime industry ran all through our family. Uncle Stephen was a Bosun, Harry was a Cook. Giddy (originally named Hilary after the actor Hilary Law whom our grandfather loved but Giddy hated the name) sailed as Chief Cook on the Booth line to Brazil. All the maritime work in Liverpool 1 was casual. They took whatever work they could find, no matter how casual. They wanted me to have a steady job '.

'I've lived and worked all over the country in Liverpool 1, Chinatown, Verulam Street, Granby, Park Lane, Everton, Bristol, Canning Street, Immingham, Anglesey, Wales and Scotland. The five kids always went on the road with us. They never came back to Liverpool. One son is in New Zealand, he's a headmaster, Carol is in Anglesey, Donna is in Nottingham, Jacqueline in Helsby and John's in London. They are all grown up now.

I live here on Dingle Grange just behind the Mount and I am quite happy. My flat looks over the communal gardens. I've been involved in many social activities with the neighbours including the running of the lottery and tontine clubs. I look out for people like we do in this family; dressing smart, boxing clever, making a living.'

John Quarless 17th July – 2018

Just A Communist Working Man

Barnaciere Musa

'I first came to Liverpool and Granby street in 1960 because the shipping company I sailed with moved up to operate out of this port.

I have always been a seaman, right from my journeys from Mombasa and Zanzibar although I was born on the Comoros Islands and taken at a very young age to Zanzibar which had formerly been incorporated into German Tanganyika.

I always lived around the port areas and very young I was taken aboard a ship which operated a mixed crew because I could speak both English and Swahili. The Chief Mate said, 'I'll take him' even though there were more experienced seamen than me waiting for the job. I have always used language to speak up for the rights of the black seafarer.

I first came to Britain in 1946 when my ship came to Hull. I met a German woman from the east of that country and we stayed together. We were living in Hull for a number of years and I was sailing out of there when an order came to deport her back to East Germany.

I went to London to fight the case. She was taken to a hostel in Ostend to prepare her for the journey east at a time when a lot of foreign nationals and ex-prisoners of war were being sent back. This was about 1952. I used to go to Hyde Park Corner every Sunday and state the unjustness of our situation from the platform. One day a man came up to me and said he was the ex- District Commissioner of Uganda and he would try and help me. Sometime later I was called to the Home Office and went with him to meet Sir David Maxwell Fyfe who was the Home Secretary. He said to me, 'I am writing this document and it says when this woman returns to London you will be married within one week. If you do not obey this condition she will be deported.

'Shall I go to Dover to meet her? I said. 'She doesn't know London.' He shook his head. 'No, she will come to you.'

I was staying with my friend on Cable Street at the time and my other friend Sam Aaronovitch used to come around and I looked out the window and saw her coming up the street, looking at every doorway to see the number. I ran out of the house and gave her a big hug.

I said, 'Did Migration say anything to you in Dover?'. She shook her head and said, 'They just gave me a red flower and your address.'

We were married next day at the church next to the registry office on the Commercial Road, a little church just past the East India Docks. I told her there was no money for rice or confetti to be thrown. I was Muslim and she was a Catholic. When we came home, Sam and his communist friends were all waiting for us and gave a party in celebration.

And I stopped sailing out of Hull when I saw the East End of London was a big shipping place. I was sailing out of London for a number of years until I came to Liverpool. I was always on the deck, an able bodied seafarer, an AB. As I say I started with the Tanganikyan Merchant Navy and always wanted to organise the seamen of east Africa because they had such a poor deal from the shipping companies.

I was a member of the NUS since I first came here in 1946 and was still a member when I retired over thirty years later in 1982 as a sailor on the Holyhead to Ireland ferry.

Before I came to Liverpool, I was on a ship to Argentina. When we arrived in Buenos Aires, there was a dock strike. The Peronist Government brought the army in. The deck crowd, us seamen, were told to operate the winches (the small ship board cranes for unloading cargo and normally operated by dockers). I told them to not do that. 'You are seamen', I said, 'and you want to go ashore tonight. What will happen when the dockers know you have been doing their jobs ? They only want a pound a day extra for food. You are robbing these men. The seamen stopped work. The First Mate came up to me and asked me what I was doing. I told him.

'Do you know who I am ?' he said. 'Of course I know who you are,' I said.

'Do you know who I am ?' he almost screamed at me. I reached up and tore the epaulettes off his uniform.

'Who are you now ?' I asked.

I was taken to the police station and questioned but the Chief of Police sent me back to the ship. The Captain called them again and said to come and take me because I was a communist troublemaker. The seamen were still not working the winches. I was taken by the police again and this time sent to prison because there was a rule there then that it was six days automatic jail for anyone who was a communist. The Captain must have found that out.

I had the best food of my life in that prison. Big steaks every day. They said at the end 'you have to pay for all your food.' I told them the Captain and the Company would pay. They brought me back to the ship. They gave me my papers and I put them in my pocket. The ship was ready to sail but I was just out of jail. I said I want to celebrate my freedom. It was a mixed crew on the deck of that ship, maybe that is why they supported me. We went to the dockers bar and had a good night and a good few drinks. The ship sailed in the morning, to Mombasa of all places. I had not been back there for over 24 years.

I was working on the deck when the Captain asked for my discharge book and passport. I told him they had not issued me with them from the jail. I had hidden them under a stack of Manilla rope. He made furious enquiries to Buenos Aires and the Company but no one could find my papers. It was my intention to get paid off when we reached Mombasa and I would need those documents. That is always the hold that the Captain on every ship has on you. They hold your State papers.

Just as we were coming alongside in Mombasa a friend of mine shouted from the quayside,'Hey Barney, there's a Harrison boat going back to Liverpool. They need an AB.' I laughed, it was one of the only jobs I refused. I wanted to stay in Mombasa. I wanted to organise all the seamen of east Africa, from Mozambique to Mogadishu. I had my documents and soon set up an office near the port, just myself and a boy.

But this was a very troubled time politically. Kenya was fighting for its independence. Kenyatta was in jail, most of the country was locked down by the British. Tom Mboya, General Secretary of the Federation of Labour and Kenyatta's Lieutenant, was responsible for the growing labour movement and introduced me to the new leader of the British TUC, George Woodcock, who was visiting at the time. He said he wanted a meeting with me. He arrived to our office and spoke with me for two hours. I sent the boy for a soft drink, that was all we had to offer him. He promised to help us. He understood the problems of the black seafarer back in Britain. But it was the Cold War and I was part of the World Federation of Trade Unions and not in the International Confederation of Free Trade Unions that was supported by the West. I was also introduced to members of MI6 who were very active at the time. They thought I could be as easily manipulated as the Sultan of Zanzibar when the Germans ruled East Africa.

George Woodcock said to me, 'How can we help? I said to him, 'I'll be deported tomorrow after these meetings.'

Next day the police came for me, white policemen who took me to see the District Commissioner. He said to me, 'who is giving you money to set up these organisations?' They thought it might have been the Chinese who liked the Kenyan Mau Mau and saw in them some of their own struggle in the countryside.

I walked back from the interview and knew my number was up. I went for a drink in the bar. People looked as if I had gone mad. There were only white people in there. The owner was sitting at the end. He nodded and the bartender served me. He asked me where I was from and I told him where I had sailed from. He said, 'I have family there'. I had another beer. White people were looking at me in the bar but it was nothing to the number outside looking in and seeing this little feller drinking beer in a white owned bar. I had my confidence up now and walked down the road and went into another bar owned by a Greek couple. They gave me a beer but told me I should not be here. I started to talk about the Greek Civil War and the Palestinians and they called the police. This time they gave me three hours to leave the country and even drove me down to the bus station where I could pick up transport back to Tanganika.

When I got there back to my country, I worked for Southern African Welfare Organisations up in the North West. The workers trade union paper in Swahili was called *Kibera* and I was involved with the editorial. I got in touch with King Street in London and asked them for thousands of the *Daily Worker* to be sent down to us. Julius Nyrere, the later President of Tanzania was involved in the trade unions at the time and gave us all the press facilities we wanted. He saw us as a beacon of trade union advancement. He was already calling the country Tanzania as it would become after independence. At this time though I was again under threat of deportation from the authorities; it was time to go back to sea again.

I came to Liverpool in 1960 and stayed here until I retired from the sea in 1982. I lived all the time in the Granby area although many of my friends and older seamen had moved up to Granby from Stanhope and the Pitt Street from around the southern docks.

When I felt black seafarers were being discriminated at the 'Pool here in Liverpool, I told a white friend what I felt was wrong. He said, 'Ok, what are you going to do about it ?' We had a series of demonstrations outside Kingston House opposite the 'Pool, the offices of the Shipping Federation and National Maritime Board, on Mann Island, saying we opposed segregation on ships. We got great support. Seamen will always turn out if they think something is not right.

The 'Pool called me in and said 'we only distribute the jobs on ships that are given to us, you'll have to go to the Company if you think you are being discriminated against.'

When I arrived to their offices, one Palm Line official said, 'the toilets are different for West African and British seamen, what will you do about that ? ' I continued to complain to the Company and got offered another Palm Line ship. I joined the ship in the South end and was met on deck by the Chief Mate. He took me down to the mess room. All the deck crew were in there. He said to them, 'Do you want to sail with him ?'

'Yeah' the reply came back,' we know him'. 'Ok,' says the Chief Mate.

I was on the eight to twelve watch and it was only 5 o'clock, so I stowed my gear in my cabin and went to the little bar, the crew had set up on the ship. Most of the deck crew were there, including the Bosun.

'What are you doing here ? 'Fuck off.' he said, 'You can sail with us but you don't come in here.' My friends stayed quiet.

I went back up on deck and then climbed up to the bridge. The Chief Mate and the Captain were there. The mate said, 'what do you want now ?' The ship was passing just off the coast at Holyhead. I said, 'I want to be put ashore there.'

The Captain almost had a heart attack, 'You want me to stop this ship?' I told him the story. He said, 'I am not stopping this ship.' I said to him, 'well I will not work until Takeradi and you can put me ashore there.'

He called the Bosun to the bridge and roared at him. Many of deck crew said they were only joking and of course I could drink at the bar. I stayed on the ship and worked all the West African coast and came back with the ship to Avonmouth. Before she arrived to Liverpool the captain called up the agent and told him to organise a new deck crew, 'I want a new crew,' he said, 'but he can stay.'

It's funny that one about Holyhead because I ended

my seagoing career on the ferry there between Wales and Dun Laoghaire in Ireland and my son Leon married a girl from around there, a Welsh speaker.

I have always been more trade union minded than political but I have played a role as Chair of the East African Welfare Federation and the North West Tanzanian Association, both charitable organisations and assisted with the exchange visits of students from East Africa that were supported by various local councils on Merseyside. When I retired from the sea, I continued to be involved in the Granby area.

This was the same with the Liverpool 8 Law Centre in Granby when I worked with Manna Brown on race relations and Maria O'Reilly, Peter Bassey and Austin Cowley from Saint Bernard's. We did some good work and there is a proposal to put all the records still held there on computer from all the struggles we engaged with in the 1980's.

I lived on Kingsley Road and Beaconsfield Street for years. Granby Street was like a town then. I have served on committees for the advancement of black people but to form any mode of co-operation you have to trust one another and sometimes there was not a great deal of trust, especially when money was concerned but we got around many issues and always tried to find a positive note.

With the four padres, Austin Cowley and Peter Morgan, whose house even now on Overbury Street is always open to refugees, John Mang and the fellow from Saint Bede's on Hartington Road whose name I can't remember, we started up the Lodge Lane Credit Union. It has been going 28 years now. Equal rights for everyone has been a key part of my life. Not just black or Chinese or Indian but equal rights for everyone no matter who they are. I was just a communist working man but you need to know your rights. Everyone needs to know that.

Outriders and Resisters

Dennis Mason

When black people first arrived in Liverpool, they settled in the Pitt Street area of St James, as historians of Liverpool's black history generally agree. They also note that during the late 1930's, 1940's and early 1950's the black community moved up the hill to what is now known as the Granby Triangle.

But there was a section of Liverpool's black community who also moved to the Granby Triangle and who, like my family in Wavertree, also   lived in places like Everton, on Brownlow Hill or Tuebrook. My earliest memories are that we were the only black family living on our street but we were not the only black family living in the area. One of the oldest black families were, to the best of my knowledge, the Coles. They lived a couple of streets away from my family and all of us children, five in number, attended the same school, Chatsworth Street County Primary, at the top end of Upper Parliament Street.

I mention this to show that not all black families lived in the Liverpool 1 or Liverpool 8 areas. One of my earliest memories is that of my mother arguing in the street with another woman because of my mother's marriage to a black African. I must have only been six or seven years of age but it is an abiding memory and that was during the middle of the 1950's.

As a child every Sunday we used to visit Uncle Nortey and his family who lived in Huyton. He was a fellow who knew my father back in Ghana and whose children we now consider to be cousins. In later years we discussed racism and they experienced much more than either my brothers' experience or my own in the city. I can vaguely recall instances of name calling but not of a racist nature, more as banter between kids, as the majority of my childhood friends were white.

When I was fourteen going on fifteen we moved to Myrtle Gardens and whilst that was not Liverpool 8, I graduated towards the L8 area and have been in love with Granby and the majority of its people ever since. The point of this short story is that not all black people moved from Pitt Street to Liverpool 8 but from several outlying districts of Liverpool.

Ropes and Dopes

Ren 'Manny' Emmanuel

'I came to Liverpool many times before finally settling here in the early 1960's from the West Indies. There was a great deal of segregation as a seaman on 'The Pool', the shipping offices on Mann Island in Liverpool. I was sanctioned many times for stating they operated a 'whites only' policy in the distribution of ships. They didn't like that.

I sailed many times with the Larrinaga Line – that at one stage took only black seamen on deck and was well known by the Pitt Street Community.

I went from Liverpool to the West Indies on Booker line ships. Bookers operated with mixed crews and I did more than ten trips with them on their ships. At one stage around this time, Bookers employed nineteen thousand workers around the West Indies and Guyana.

I was always a straight talker and when I found a Captain and a Bosun selling rope, I reported them. They in turn accused me of stealing. I was hauled before the courts but they cleared me. It was like that with practices aboard ship at that time. They did it with drink in the so called 'Captain's Bond.' The rope was used for tethering horses on the 'cattle boats', the seaman's and the animals' lives were made the worse for the lack of it especially in 'heavy ' weather.

I lived on Selbourne Street and I knew the clubs on Parliament Street and Princes Avenue. I used to eat out all the time on Granby Street when I was home. After the Larrinaga line I shipped out with Lamport and Holt and Blue Funnel Lines. I worked all the islands between Japan, Manilla and Bangkok. Those ships were all mixed on deck except the Blue Funnel. They used to have all the Chinese seamen down below.

As a West Indian seaman, firmly settled in Liverpool, I wouldn't ship out with the Harrison line who employed many black seamen. They were 'cheap' ships who only paid the seamen the least rate possible. They were also known as 'Hungry' from their reputation during the Depression. Even their hooped funnels were known as 'two of fat and one of lean'.

I lived on Grove Street when I was going away for the Lamport and Holt line and worked the ports of Trinidad, Gulf of Mexico and Latin America via the Panama Canal. In my early days as a boy seaman sailing out of the West Indies I was encouraged to come to Liverpool by other West Indian, mainly Jamaican. sailors who had settled in the Granby Street area. Gurley Jones from Trenchtown was the one who mainly encouraged me to come and stay.

I had been sailing for ten years between Jamaica and New York and had my AB's ticket. In the States, the ships were full of smuggling gangs running between New York and New Orleans. Many of the seamen carried guns. The FBI had trailed one ship, the *Ipsacros* down the whole of the East Coast. It wasn't until Baton Rouge in Louisiana that they nailed who they were looking for. Three of my ship mates got jail sentences from that raid.

There was so much smuggling going on that it was difficult to sometimes know what to do for the best. One time, stupidly, I took a mate's sea bag ashore for him, a fellow seaman in the port of Galveston who was intent on jumping the ship , the *Alula Green*. The FBI picked me up at the same time as they were following him. Generously the Captain pledged my good conduct to them and took me back aboard again and signed my bond so that I wouldn't have to go to jail. The jails in Galveston and Houston were bad places. I'll never forget that generous act. What a kind man, that Captain Cook was. The southern states were terrible back then for segregation, I think a lot of the smuggling was done just as opposition or resistance to that oppression. I never went ashore in South Africa, you could see what was happening there.

After the American coast I worked with the Sun Line that shipped out of Montreal. That's when I made Bosun and came to Liverpool on the ship the *Sun Valley*. I had been coming to Liverpool since 1960 but I did not settle here until some years later. I lived all around the Granby area but mainly on Selborne Street when I finally settled.

In Liverpool in the Seaman's strike of 1966, our crew was paid off in the West Indies. By the time the strike finished we all had to be flown back out to re- join the ship. This cost the company a fortune. The Captain was demoted to First Mate when the ship returned to Liverpool. Ships in the strike were allowed to sail back to their home port, providing they tied up there on arrival. I often wonder whatever happened to that 'Captain'.

Granby was an easy place to live and to go out, the same way as New York was easy and the Islands and across to Africa, to Takeradi, Port Harcourt, Freetown, on the African Coast. Club after club after club, with no one to bother you, a seaman's life could be good sometimes.

Most of the people I knew were seamen. Don't forget I was most of my life at sea and only packed it in when I was 63. All my children are in Liverpool and I have five grandchildren, three in Liverpool, one in London and one in the USA.

All this time you have asked me only about ships and

where I sailed, where I went and where I stayed, what I did and what I didn't do. I could tell you as much about Granby Street as I have done about ships. We used to have some laughs there in those clubs.'

We Had A Laugh

Rose Thomas

My parents and grandparents all came from Beaufort Street and Stanhope Street above the southern docks. I was born and brought up on Upper Parliament Street. My grandfather had nine kids. I don't know what he did, he could have been a docker, but the eldest, Sammy, worked on the bins. You didn't know then what your grandparents did then, they just worked. He had been a seaman.

My mum and her little gang used to go searching for food, they would steal biscuits and milk from the diary. They took her into care when she was nine, her and her little mates. They put her in a home miles away so no one could visit her. She spent seven years in care but she came out with a trade. She was a tailoress and she was a good one. Us kids were always well turned out.

She met my father through a friend on Stanhope Street. He was staying down there. She married young at 18. He was a qualified chemist and had been to university. I remember one letter she told me about when he applied to one of the big medical supply companies in Liverpool.

It read, 'Dear Mr Thomas thank you for your application but we regret we have no openings for witch doctors on our team at present.' It hurt him deeply. He worked for many years as a bricklayer and then later in life at Pilkingtons at Saint Helens as a low grade technician.

His son, my brother Sammy was sent to Africa at the age of twelve and he became a chemist. He came home some years later and studied at Liverpool University. He then returned to Nigeria where he practised as a chemist all his life. I think he did it for my dad. He really wanted to be a vet. He's 77 now, two years older than me and is living a happy retirement outside of Lagos.

My father was a devoted man. He never drank or smoked. He bought his own house on Upper Parliament Street when the man who we were renting off offered to sell it to us provided he could keep an office upstairs. Sadly Mr Baker was murdered just a couple of years later in the late 1950's, when I was fifteen. My mother was a munitions officer in the second war and my dad an air raid warden. When he retired he also went back to Africa and opened a chemist's shop in the country. People who could pay, paid; people who could not, did not. He was a real man of the people, my dad. He died happy in Africa.

Quite late in life he became a welfare officer for all the Nigerian officers that were starting to sail on ships affiliated to Elder Dempster. He flew all around Europe to the various ports, looking after their welfare. He was very strict but fair. I think that is the reason he did not send me to Africa. He knew I would hate the disciple there and the rough treatment meted out. He used to say 'Rose stays here, it suits her' and Granby was such a laugh with all the music and the clubs in the 1960's. He died in Lagos. He was a wonderful person my dad.

But I don't want to be too one sided here, my mother was great as well but she wasn't easy. She was the stronger of the two of them. She kept things going. He went along with her. She was very ambitious and she pulled him into her ambition. She ran a little club called 'The Hole in the Wall' up in Everton during the war. You know, for the GI's. She had little illicit drinks in small bottles and glasses of lemonade. He never knew. He was just a softy but she was very good and pulled him along with her.

He came from Stanhope Street where the Elder Dempster Company had a hostel for black seamen who sailed their ships. He brought culture to our family. He always encouraged us to read. I always remember him taking us kids everywhere. We used to go to the cartoon shows at the Tatler in Clayton Square and I can still hear him laughing now. My brother in law ended up as a captain of merchant ships sailing out of West Africa, among them Elder Dempster. My sister met him when he came to study for his tickets in Liverpool.

Africa would have been too strict for me. I remember my older brother's first letters home at the age of twelve, how he loved the country, being outside, climbing trees and running free. Then he went to the Christian Brothers boarding school up in the north of the country with the Hausa people and how he used to complain of the strictness, the shouting , the 'hands on' discipline and treatment by the teachers. He was the one who came back here to study. He laughed about it then but he didn't like it at first. He still went back to Africa though, he said, 'you know where you are there'.

I can understand that now. In Liverpool when you look at the kids and you hear tales of the guns and the knives for any little disturbance. It used to be just a little bit of weed but it's a lot more serious than that now. Look at these latest series of killings. A lot of the kids just don't know who they are and just start waving a gun around.

I lived all around Granby from Upper Parley, Amberley Street, Jermyn Street, then down in London. Dancing and partying all through the 1960's. That was my time. Granby Street was just part of my party.

But there was sadness too, I let my first daughter go

back to British Guyana with her father from the age of 5 till she was 12, I always regretted that. Letting her go killed me but I thought I was doing it for the best. When she came back, a sulky teenager, life was difficult at first but then it got better and we are very close now.

My other daughter, Erica sadly died in Alder Hey at the age of 14, in 1984. Her death left me heartbroken to the point where I was unable to deal with my eleven year old son's emotional needs. Something happened in that year because it was very difficult to access medical records there and I wasn't able to fully access inquest reports till 2001 and by that time it was too late, 'timed out' to make any appeal. I finally received a letter from the City Council in 2011 where they apologised for the language used in the original report in 1984 where Erica was described as a 'negro' but it didn't matter much by then, what was gone was gone.

Her death had the greatest effect on my son who was eleven at the time and got 'lost' in the whole process. It was a very unsettled time for him and as he searched for what was lost he got in with some youngsters with similar backgrounds to his own. You could easily do that on Granby in the 1980's. I put it down to a search for himself. He's a different person now and our Tracy has five grandchildren of her own and they all come to see me. The youngest one came through the front door and just said 'Wow'. She was looking at all the worthless antiques that make up a grandmother's home.

I said, 'welcome to a black woman's house.'

Both my kids are very strong and I am grateful for that. I was a nurse for many years and worked at the Women's on Catherine Street. I would have stayed and got more qualified but when you have a young baby and you are a single mother, you don't always see what's best for you, the immediacy of life takes over, house cleaning, food on the table and all the other things you need to keep going. It was only later when I started attending courses and getting educated that I could see things clearer for a young single woman of 21 and one with a child to look after.

Warren came to a reading of the book I am just completing and he stood up and said he was very proud of me. That felt good. And it felt good to say to the little one, 'welcome to a black woman's house' not just for me but for both my mother and grandmother because life was a struggle for them. This is where it comes full circle. I am seventy five now and on the way out but when I sit down with my friends, we always laugh. I say I have had a wonderful life and I've had a laugh and laughter defines us no matter who we are.

The Man in the Trilby Hat

Mary Alker

The sun shone through the window allowing a hazy warm mist to enter a room within the tall Victorian house on Ponsonby Street that my dad had rented out. It wasn't unlike the rooms he had rented before in other houses around the Granby Street area, except this one seemed much quieter. He wouldn't stay long in that room before another ship would draw him back to the sea.

I was sitting on the carpeted floor opposite my Dad as he shared out the ivory domino set between us; one by one we matched up the black dots on the set. Other than the clinking together of the pieces it was quiet apart from the occasional 'Hmm,' Dad would murmur before making his next move.

The curtains were semi drawn, shading us from the stifling heat as the afternoon sun grew stronger. The game had ended. Dad leaned back in his armchair and closed his eyes. His legs stretched out in front of him, he hugged the newspaper, which was opened at the sports page, to his chest. I lay on top of his bed studying him before I drifted off.

It felt like I had been asleep for some time but it had only been twenty minutes or so. It was the sound of an excited man's voice shouting from the radio that woke me. Dad was listening out for his horse in the two-thirty race.

Leaning over to the mantelpiece where he kept his pipes, I watched dad as he ran his fingers across them. I made a bet with myself which one he would choose. He had a small selection of silver, ivory and wooden stemmed pipes. He usually went for the wooden pipe and sure enough after hesitating, he opted for the wooden one as I had predicted.

He blew into the fat end of the pipe to clear away any dust then began stuffing it with tobacco.

Flipping the lid of his silver lighter he flicked it a few times until the flint caught light producing a large blowtorch-like flame. Angling it towards his pipe he sucked hard on the stem and the tobacco sizzled, glowing under the hot flame with every suck as he puffed out smoke from the corner of his mouth. The misty room now smelt of sweet Cavendish tobacco, a distinct comforting aromatic smell that would remind me of Dad years later.

Mumbling something to me, Dad drew the curtains back. My eyes screwed from the full glare of the sun. I smiled to give acknowledgment but didn't have a clue what he said. That was part of our relationship - Dad spoke softly almost whispering in a broken English accent that he had adopted. Sometimes I understood, but not very often - dialogue wasn't a natural part of our relationship. Instead we shared smiles that sometimes made me feel unfamiliar or awkward, as if we were strangers. Apart from the love I felt, I never knew much else about my dad, except that he came in and out of my life for most of it.

The strong aroma of cumin wafted around the communal kitchen. Dad lit the stove to reheat the soup. The gas hissed out a blue flame under the pan until the soup bubbled. This was Dad's famous 'See through' soup as I had aptly named it. It was made up of potatoes, lamb chops and tomatoes. It amazed me how Dad managed to cook the ingredients yet they remained separate holding their place at the bottom of the bowl with the liquid smelling fragrantly sitting on top so that you could see right through to the bottom, hence the name. I tried to copy his recipe years later and although the flavour was a match, which was little more than cumin, salt and pepper, the potatoes turned into mush making it look more like a thick stew despite my efforts. I am glad of my persistence to try to master it nonetheless because the soup remains one of Dad's legacies.

After ripping the flesh of the lamb and slurping the hot liquid, Dad put his jacket on and I brushed the front of my new lemon and green dress that dad had bought me for my eighth birthday a week earlier, before we retired back into his room.

The armchair creaked with age and wear until Dad made himself comfortable. Pulling out his tortoiseshell comb he began grooming his moustache for a while before pinching together his middle finger and thumb placing them in the centre of his moustache and slowly parting them so that they extended to both sides of his face. Over and over he stroked his moustache with his eyes transfixed on the space in front of him, lost in his thoughts as if forgetting I was there. Walking over to his dressing table, he pulled out a stick from his white tin mug that had a navy blue rim. The stick was about ten inches long. Dad began to chew the end until it was soft then he rubbed it over his teeth, over and over again. I heard him chewing and sucking at the stick and watched as he went off into another long trance.

It was nearly time for me to go home. I hated leaving dad and I worried myself about his possible loneliness. I thought about returning home to our mad house full of us kids running around playing and mum shouting. It was so tranquil at dad's… when I leave he would be alone in this room. My throat hurt as I tried to swallow back my tears. How long would it be before I would see my Dad again?

As if he had read my mind, Dad took hold of my hand and placed it palm up cradling it in his. Circling his finger around my palm over and over again, he spoke in his native tongue, it sounded funny and made me giggle. He chased his fingers up my arm and tickled me under my armpit. I rolled about laughing each time until my ribs hurt. Eventually he would stop and we would go back to our silence.

After putting his shoes on he took out his shoeshine kit and began to run the blackened cloth across his already immaculate polished shoes. He grabbed his summer overcoat and scarf. I don't ever remember seeing dad dressed in any other way but this. I had never seen him in casual clothing and I couldn't help but wonder if he dressed like this when receiving visitors? It wasn't until years later that it occurred to me that perhaps dad was just trying to fit into a new world so different from his own.

Standing in front of the mirror that hung over the fireplace, Dad held his trilby hat. He began to play with the brim brushing off some unseen fluff, and then squeezing the creases with his fingers he reshaped it before finally placing it on his head just so. 'Come,' he said taking hold of my hand very delicately as if it was made out of the best china. My visit over, we began to stroll down the street heading towards the bus stop.

It was almost five o'clock and the tarmac on the road looked like melting treacle glistening under the early evening sun. Shops were putting up their boards ready to close up for the day. Young lads wearing no shirts leaned on walls whistling at the girls passing by, mothers chatted to one another as their children circled them for amusement, twisting and pulling at their skirts until they were shouted at and ordered to stop. Another child was holding onto a pushchair, crying hysterically as his mummy ignored his pleas and walked straight past the sweetshop.

Some women walked slowly, heads held high, proudly wearing colourful native costume with matching scarves wrapped around their heads. Others shuffled along in aprons and slippers, wearing scarves to cover curlers. A few men were sitting outside a café playing cards, others went in and out of the betting shop with bits of yellow or pink paper in their hands, one man screwed the paper up and threw it to the ground on his way out.

The smell of spices mixed with the sweetness of candy- floss and cigarette smoke filled the air, it was mesmerising. The atmosphere was bustling and happy. I heard lots of different languages being spoken all at once. It was rare to see so many black people. This was a whole different world, a world I didn't understand and part of me was scared.

Stopping for a moment Dad squeezed my hand as if sensing my trepidation. I looked at him and saw sadness behind his eyes. 'You are my favourite,' he said as clear as daylight. It wasn't my imagination, those were his words. I froze and held his gaze searching his face, waiting for him to speak again, but he never. Instead, he gently stroked my cheek. It felt as if this would be the last time I would ever see him again.

My heart melted like an ice cream under a scorching sun. My eyes welled. I had no control over the emotions that came gushing out wetting my new dress. I didn't want to leave my Daddy. I wanted him to come home with me. I wanted to take care of him and I didn't want him to be sad. I didn't want my Dad to miss me.

I tried to wipe my tears and snotty nose with the back of my hand. Instead I made a right muckiness all over my face. Dad knelt down pulling out a clean handkerchief and wiped away my mess before giving me a hug. I sniffled while trying to suck air but started to splutter and cough. 'Shh' Dad whispered to me until I eventually felt calm and secure in his arms. Eventually we resumed our walk towards the bus stop, my small hand holding onto his cold hand, as we continued our journey in a sorrowful quietness.

The sadness was shortly relieved by a visit to the sweetshop. I emerged with: a lucky bag, chocolate bar and fizzy drink, along with a brand new crispy ten-pound note that Dad had folded into my hand closing it really tight as he did so.

Flagging down a passing taxi Dad knelt down and we gave one another a tight hug and kiss before I was placed onto the back seat and the driver given money to see me home safely. We waved until my dad grew smaller into the distance until the only thing that resembled my dad was his paisley scarf blowing in the warm summer breeze.

Cops 'n Shops

Dennis Mason

Granby Street itself and some of the characters who shopped, worked, played, lived and died there formulated some of my happiest and saddest memories.

From hanging around Halletts cake shop, to sitting in one of the cafés or watching some of my friends breaking sprint records, while being chased by Jock Lang from Essex Street police station or hiding from one or both of their parents, having committed some minor infraction and trying to avoid the consequences, forgetting that they would have to go home sometime or later. It all provided a great memory.

The Granby Street of my youth was not just somewhere to shop, it was a meeting place. It was somewhere that you could buy anything or see somebody, as sooner or later they would all appear on Granby Street.

Tesco had a long established presence on the Street as far back as the 1960's. Some say it was the first one in Liverpool but it's long gone now. Granby Street was the heart and soul of the South End of Liverpool as it was unofficially known. Here there were jewellers, a post office and chandlers, one of the original mini markets (Bashir's) where you could buy anything. Granby also had a cinema, cafés, clubs, fish shops (Harold's), second hand shops, a dairy and a school. Granby had everything that a community would need. Granby had it all.

For me and others of my age group being brought up in the South End (L8) and mixing with different nationalities and races was the norm. Africans, West Indians, Yemenis, Norwegians, Americans, Chinese,

Malayans, being surrounded by all these different nationalities and hearing different languages and accents was a great way to learn about the world, without leaving Liverpool 8. You didn't need to go into the City Centre if you didn't want to, you had it all here.

Equality and Diversity (even if it wasn't called that in the 1960's) was practised on Granby Street. I can recall a shop keeper, Mr Smith (honest), who had a disabled arm but that didn't prevent him from taking your money and tossing it into the till using his disabled hand. Then there was Mr Blye who was so opinionated and thought he knew everything. He owned a second hand shop on Granby and the rooms above he rented out as accommodation. There was a lot of that then. Harold the fishmonger was on Granby more years than I can remember.

One of my earliest memories of Granby Street was standing on the corner of Granby when it still met Upper Parliament Street. It was outside a club (I think it was the Ibo or might have been the Nigerian) selling copies of a magazine called the West African for a shilling. How I got conned into that by my dad, I will never know.

All The Way From Canada

Norman Kowalsky

I was born in Hatherley Street in circa 1942. The middle of three children. Ruth my elder sister, 'Bunny' my younger brother.

Growing up in Hatherley Street, just after the war. We were all poor, and we didn't know it. In the Granby triangle it was a very cosmopolitan mixture of people, even at that time. All in the same boat, poor with mouths to feed.

At this time there were very few people of African descent in our area. There were pockets, in North Hill Street, a few families in Selborne Street and then Hatherley Street. In the 1940's, that was all the African descended families in our area.

To name the families that lived in Hatherley Street is easy. You see we were all mates. The Knowles Family; Johnny Quanita, Pauline, Leon, Nathaniel, Josephine. The Williams Family; Eddie Franklin. The Adgecumbe Family; Elliot, Sylvia and Sydney. There was Tony Williams. There was Tommy Edwards. Also there was Chris and Kevin Dawala.

We, at this time grew up as a close knit family, we would go into their homes, they would come into our homes. If food was offered, it was mainly a bread and marge butty, from both sides, as that was all we could afford.

If fights occurred, it was other children from other streets, Ponsonby, Eversley, Rosebery, or Northbrook, looking to pick a fight with any of the above mentioned families. Plus I managed to get into a few scrapes on my own - I wasn't pristine. We children from Hatherley Street, all stood toe to toe at this time. We never saw the different skin colour in our street neighbours - these were all mates.

On the corner of Hatherley Street at Mulgrave Street, was painted a goal post on the wall; during summer holidays, football would be played on this corner for hours by us boys. Girls would skip rope, play ball or hopscotch, or swing on a rope around a lamppost (no TV); no one at this time could afford a bike even.

At 10 years old I went to work for Waterworths Greengrocer, on the corner of Hatherley and Granby, delivering produce to homes, Friday evening and all day Saturday. (I was stopped by school board, because I was too young.) At 12, I went to work for Roberts the butcher. Again on Granby Street. This is where l lose a bit of the history. My job at Roberts was from 8am-9am, 12.30pm-1.30pm and then from 4pm till 5.30pm all week and all day Saturday. I did this for just over three years. I left Granby Street School at 15. I also left Roberts. l had several jobs. Marfac Greenland Street, Bells Gascoyne Street. Eventually l ended up doing construction work.

l was on the crew that excavated the foundation for the St Johns Tower in 1965. Various construction jobs in and around Liverpool and its environs. In 1970 construction work dried up in Liverpool. I had to travel out of town for employment. I worked various construction jobs in the areas of York, London, Southampton, Newcastle, and Dunoon Scotland.

In 1975 I successfully applied to emigrate to Canada, where l built a very successful life. l retired as a high ironworker and welder. YES up there, way up there on the high steel beams and girders, l worked on the roof of the CN Tower when it was under construction in 1975.

Granby Street School was where l learnt my education. There were 40 children in our boys only class. The whole four senior years at school, we had TWO teachers, Mr Melcher, and Mr Kirby. Both teacher's very firm, but fair. Our Head Master was a Mr Koppack, also firm and fair. If you screwed up at school, you were caned, if your mum got to know you received a caning at school, you would, as Cilla sang 'get a belt from your dad'. I can still almost recall all the names on the register as it was read out each morning during my school years. My young brother, Bunny, and I were good friends with Tony and Michael Showers when we were young children, visiting each other's homes. Tony was in my class at Granby along with Sol Bassey and Jake Abrahams.

The Granby class of '57 had a huge meet up about ten years ago. l travelled over from Canada to attend. There were approx. 37 both boys and girls showed up for this reunion in the Weatherspoons bar in Charlotte Street. Most of our class, even though we were only given the barest of education, every one there, at Weatherspoons, had made it, through hard graft.

Granby Street was a street full of shops and it also had a cinema, The Princes Theatre. There were shops of every description the length of Granby Street. There were THREE Co-ops, a grocery store, a butchers store and a dairy next to the school. There were three Waterworths greengrocers on Granby. Harrowby Street, Hatherley Street and Arundel Street. There were three dairies, with live cows along Granby Street. Sunters in Selbourne Street, another in Eversley Street and a third in Cawdor Street.

Bakers and chip shops, chandlers and cobblers,

hairdressers and newsagents, tobacconists and sweetshops. Junkshops (Swainbanks), false teeth makers, even a building merchant on the corner of Eversley, facing Hilda's the dress shop. Goodalls was another dress shop on Granby Street.

It was a very vibrant area when I lived there until 1975. Time and riots erode buildings and memories. I walked down the length of Granby last year. I was stared at, maybe these newbies thought I was a stranger. Alas, if they only knew.

Four Women of Faith

Marie Gray

This is my memory of four women of faith. I did not grow up in Granby, but I want to tell you about four special friends whose shared memories, and the telling of them, have helped to form the happy memories of many people – growing up in Granby.

> Molly Amero, Born 1911, now in 104th year
> Lil Clarke, Born 1914, now in 101st year
> Madge Prior, Born and lived in Granby for 98 years
> Mary Byrne, Lived in Granby for 92 years

Those who lived in those streets alongside Lil, Mary, Madge and Molly will testify to them being four cornerstones, four women of faith.

Lil, widowed in the war, her sister Mary, with friends Madge and Molly had taught many girls - no boys then - to sing, dance and put on concerts and plays. The front room in Cawdor Street was the rehearsal room, with Mary's husband Joe on the piano. These 'girls', in their 60s now, still meet on occasions – lifelong friends, sharing happy memories of their younger days in and around Cawdor Street.

Aged 100 years now, Lil still encourages her visitors to join her in a song, usually a popular hymn. Her eyesight may be failing, her voice as strong as ever. Well into her older age she continued to attend weekly choir practice, a firm believer in lifelong learning to keep up her skills!

Mary, a seamstress in those days, had taught the girls how to sew, and later was to make the wedding dresses for their marriages at St Bernard's. Many of these brides attended Mary's 90th Birthday party, staging an exhibition of their wedding photos. In fact most of their activities centred on St Bernard's, their faith playing an important part in the lives of the four friends.

Lil says that Molly was the 'more educated and reserved' of the friends. She did not sing but wrote plays and acted in sketches. Molly had a great faith in young people, and the need for older people to support and encourage the young. At aged nearly 80 years, she was still volunteering in Granby School, helping the children with reading. Molly has reached 103 years old now, recently being joined in her care home by the younger, 100 year old Lil Clarke, no doubt recalling scenes from their younger days.

Fame came when the four friends entered the National Pensioners' Talent Competition and won, but then they'd had much practice entertaining residents in local care homes, since 'many old people don't get any visitors', at a time when they themselves were all over 80!

Madge was Lil's special friend and also widowed quite young. Madge had lived in the same house in Cawdor Street where she was born over 98 years earlier, and which was to be knocked down. Heartbroken, she accepted the need for progress, and although being told she would be allocated a house in the new Cawdor Street, Madge did not make her 100 years, but passed away at her daughter's home, aged 99.

Four faithful friends, faithful to St Bernard's, faithful to each other, faithful to their community, faithful to their memories, faithful to Granby.

The Little Mosque

Higah Baggash

My name is Higah Baggash. I have been here in Granby Street about 52 years and I had a shop around the corner. It was a really nice place. There used to be a post office near us, and you had a laundrette and a bakery in Granby Street, and we had vegetable shops and a fish market and you really bought locally, so it was lovely for us. Then my children grew up on that road, we did not want to go anywhere, we love and wanted to stay in that area. I was very confident in that area. There were really good neighbours to us. People shared everything.

There used to be a Mosque on Friday nights inside my house, this was when I first bought it 52 years ago. I no longer have the Mosque as there are too many people, we all go to the big one that has been built.

There was a school in the basement as well in my house, teaching people. Children would come on a Saturday. This was before my children were born. My father-in-law was an Imam and he lived in the house with us. My husband would do teaching and would help with the translations for those that could not speak English. He was very good speaking English, mine is very bad. Liverpool was the first place I came to when I came to the UK.

My husband lived here with his father, who had lived here since before I was born, since the First World War. My husband came to our country to marry me and then brought me back here. My Uncle was a Seaman in the Second World War and had come to live here also.

There was only a small number of us living here at

that time and they would gather together. This is how I came to be with my husband.

I have seen lots of changes. I wish it was the same, that it hadn't changed in Granby. It was nicer back then. Life was so much easier.

Community Friends

Mary Baillie

I was an incomer here in 1976, nearly 40 years ago and I didn't know a soul in Liverpool 8 when I moved here. Granby Street was a thriving shopping centre then. I had found a house in Cawdor Street, but couldn't get the deposit together in time before a young couple did. Anyway, around Lodge Lane, I found a home on Lime Grove, where I still live.

The Lodge Lane East Residents Association was in full swing then. I joined it and got to know Margaret B here (not so much of her in those days). She was one of the key voluntary workers, along with Mrs Pine and Edna and Pat Finnerly. I wish we had something like it now. It had been started up, I think, by a paid community worker, Tony Hood.

Margaret was active raising funds for outings for the children and the pensioners. She organised the 5-a-side football team and was a cycling enthusiast. Alan Geddis and his wife at the Chaplins pub were involved and there was a very sociable atmosphere.

Lodge Lane was like Granby, a busy shopping street. Things changed after the civil disturbances, in 1981, the riots. I had a job at Princes Park Hospital then, which was an NHS residential home for the elderly at the time. Martha was also working there at that time.

The residents were all taken by taxi on the first night of the rioting and there was a danger of fire at the home when the Rackets Club next door was torched. A truce was negotiated to allow the safe transfer of the residents.

I got to know more local people through the hospital,

also through becoming a member of St Margaret's church which was behind the home. I'm still a member - I met some of the African Caribbean community through the church. I also met Father Peter Morgan at St Bernard's. Race relations were all in the mix of the 1981 riots.

Things move on and now the Muslim communities have settled in the Granby and Lodge Lane areas. Lodge Lane is busy again with Muslim shops, cafes, social centres, language centres and barbers. The last two families who have lived next door to me have been immigrant families from Sudan and very friendly.

My friendship with Margaret and her family has grown stronger, now we've both been retired for some time from our paid jobs - I've learned so much from her and her love of Granby and Lodge Lane. There is still something here, some sense of community which is full of memories but also the new, the future.

Margaret's Poems

I have lived in Liverpool 8 since my childhood and my days were spent in Granby Street School from 1947 till 1957. I'm a great fan of Elvis the King. I went to Graceland in 2002 and it's a memory I will always treasure. In the past I worked as a volunteer for a Residents Association and Play Schemes. We ran pensioners outings and days out for the children. Those children are grown up now and they say they always remember those days. LLERA United was the name we called the football team I ran from the Lodge Lane East Residents Association. Here are some of my poems.

Childhood Days

Margaret Berrington

Sometimes when I am on my own
I think of my early childhood home
The days when I was young and carefree
With nothing in the world to bother me

When going to school you thought it great
And being in bed for half past eight
To get up early in plenty of time
Because school started dead on nine

When school finished you'd go straight home
So Mother would have no reason to moan
Playing with friends content you would be
Till it was time to go in for tea

When bedtime came dear Mother was there
To kiss us goodnight and say a prayer
Though I was wild and also free
This was my home where I loved to be

But childhood days go quickly it seems
And now I see them only in dreams
I've grown up now a family of my own
I'll never forget my childhood home

My School

Margaret Berrington

Granby Street School was very special to me
I spent my days there young and free
The making of new friends you would find
And they certainly were one of a kind

The teachers in them days were very good
Helping you to do the best you could
You'd have fun in the yard of playtime
When the whistle blew you'd stand in line

Then you would go back to your classroom
Knowing that your teacher would be coming soon
Your lessons would start what will they be
It could be maths or even on history

We had cooking lessons I wasn't so good
But always did the best that I could
I was very good in sport so they would say
And that certainly did make my day

Granby Street School were strict but fair
And I really did enjoy my time there
My memories of this school were a pleasure
And something that I will always treasure

Granby

Margaret Berrington

Granby Street was a brilliant area years ago
When off to the shops that you'd know
We had the butchers and the bakers
And even a Tesco to where you'd go

We had Leffras the sweet shop
Across the road from the school
And Shettlers the dairy
Where things were cool

The laundrette where you got
Your washing done
And talking to friends as time
Moved on

We even had a cinema in Granby Street
And watching the matinees there it was a treat
They called it the Bug House it didn't bother me
When it finished I'd go home for tea

Many other shops in Granby Street too
I've just happened to mention a few
But they're all gone now I'm sad to say
It's just a shame they couldn't stay

They've built houses around there now
As you can see
But one thing they can't take
Is our Community

Maria's Poems

I am a great grandmother, passionate about civil rights
and racial justice, a lifelong community activist. Here are
some of my poems.

Granby

Maria O'Reilly

Why were you there
the young man said

I was there out of love and pride

Shared history was mine
Generations gone by
left a legacy I share
Injustice not despair
like a whip across my back made me move forward
here was no turning back

Strength out of unity L8
That's why I was there
taking part in history
I was not alone
my ancestors legacy
belonged to others like me
The struggle for justice wasn't just mine
the hunger for equality belongs to us all

A powerful idea came down the line
it landed in Granby
shared history was mine
That's why I was there
at that point, at that time

Liverpool 8

Maria O'Reilly

Just a place called Granby Ward
intertwined black and white

lots of memories of times gone by
communities moved on and out

Memories of struggle which left a legacy
stories untold of sheroes and heroes
not given a mention

Remembering how Granby was
brave and put up a fight
many can claim a part of this stage
whether young or old
black or white

We stood against racism and prejudice
always remember Granby has struggled for what is right

We had laughter and comradeship
We built from grassroots
projects, business and clubs
now gone, raised to the floor

The managed decline of those regarded as poor
we did this to provide solutions to problems we saw

We don't need a housing estate to be gentrified
We need a community built on who we are with pride

Pride in our achievements
Keep Granby alive
Its history intact
this way a future will be built on the fact

Granby is legend
The heart of our soul
Strength out of unity L8
a positive view before it's too late

Martha Said

Maria O'Reilly

Martha said there were things
that were wrong we had to put right

Many a struggle by everyone
coming together made Granby a
place we are proud to be from

Martha said there were things
that were wrong we had to put right

We had to be heard
so we did not whisper
or turn back with fright

Martha said there were things
that were wrong we had to put right

We found a voice deep from our
roots, which roared out loudly
can still be heard now

Martha said there are things
that are wrong and we have to put them right

Lyn's Story

Lyn Bayack, Hector Peterson Court

I came from Cardiff with my family. My husband was from Trinidad and went away to sea. Granby Street used to be the place to meet friends, do your shopping. We had no reason to go into the city. We had everything we wanted right on our doorstep. We have been waiting a long time for Granby to be built up again, always promises.

I am nearly 83 years old and hope it can recover from all it's been through. The people need to get together regardless of race or religion, like one another, understand each other's way of life. Granby is the heart of Toxteth, let our hearts beat as one, and it will be great again. Let's make the next generation proud. I may not be here to see it happen but it will I'm sure.

Has anyone asked the young people how they would like to see Granby? I'm sure they would like to have a say in what will happen.

Jeanette's Story

Jeanette Martin, Hector Peterson Court

I was born in 1948 on Kingsley Road and soon after we moved to Hatherley Street. I remember on Granby - I attended the nursery there in the early 1950's - I remember the Post Office, the chemist's, the chandler's, the jeweller's, the fish shops, the bread shop where you bought homemade bread, Goodalls the clothes shops, the paraffin heater shop, the Jewish shops and Chinese laundry, Ali Beshir's (Norma's) the butcher, Hilda's shoe shop, Merriman's the other butcher, the police station that was never open, the Arab man had a wholesalers and the black guy who kept the dairy.

My mother was a domestic cleaner and my father was a sea going fireman who was from South Africa, I remember dad bringing elephant tusks home and the big old house we used to live in. It was full of souvenirs from when he went to sea. He would sit me on his knee and tell me stories of all the oceans; a big strong working fireman.

I've worked all over Liverpool, in Walkers factory and a bakery in Aigburth, in Jacobs at Aintree and at a confectioners in Woolton. A group of us from Granby used to go down and work the summers at Butlins in Pwllheli.

I didn't really go to the clubs regularly but I remember the dances in the Caribbean Centre and attending ceremonies at the Freetown and the Sierra Leone on Princes Avenue. The Nigerian, where you had to go down the stone steps to get in and where all my dad's mates used to go. I have lived with six families in my life and all of them have been good to me but I still remember my dad's stories.

Halima's Story

Halima Mohammed, Hector Peterson Court

My mother was white and my father was black. My husband was a fireman and he later worked on the Dredgers. He came from a family with more money than ours. We lived in the first house on Ponsonby Street and we opened a shop. We bought a grocery shop and then we opened a dairy. We had a café and lived above it and we could hear all the Somali seamen playing cards below. My mother, Mary Fletcher was pure Irish and married a Somali Seaman. Her parents disowned her. My mother and father went on to have nineteen children including myself. We weren't a family, we were an empire. There was no money but we were all loved.

There were thousands of shops on Granby Street at the time. Lord Woodbine had a second hand clothes shop. Compulsory Purchase Orders (CPO's) drove the population and then the businesses away. They say that the newer population of Somalis and Yemenis are different from the older residents of Granby, but they are not. They have the same issues. I talk with many of them about their sons and daughters.

Conversations at Lodge Lane Women's Somali Group

Madeline Heneghan visited the Lodge Lane Somali Women's group during a morning session attended by elders. The women were getting ready for a much anticipated armchair aerobics class and there was time for an informal chat about their experiences and perceptions of the Granby area and hopes for its future. The women spoke in Somali while Asha Shiren, a younger woman, translated the conversation.

The women came to settle here between 1985 and 2014. Many came to escape the civil war that raged in their homeland, sponsored by relatives who could trace their family presence in Granby to the men who had settled here as Seafarers.

Hawo, an older woman, described how she first emigrated from Somalia to the Netherlands but came to join her sister here. She felt the social opportunities for her in Liverpool were much greater than those in Holland. Asha came in 1986 and her husband secured employment in Ford. She felt Granby Street to be a little dangerous back then. But now it feels like there are more Somali families and it is a very good and safe area to live.

Isir arrived in 1995 but her family had been resident in Liverpool since the 1960's. Halima came to Liverpool in 2001 and remembers Granby Street as having one or two shops; Danny's and Nabil's. She felt it was much better now that new shops were opening.

When asked what would improve the Granby area, all women indicated that a market square would greatly improve and energise the community.

Madeline had a one to one conversation with voluntary worker Fatima. Fatima has lived in the Granby area for 28 years. She joined her husband and brother from Somaliland when she was 24 years old. Her husband and brother were both seafarers, recruited to the merchant navy in Somalia, she thinks. Her husband has served with the Auxiliary fleet during the Falklands war and has journeyed to South Africa and Japan. She remembers when she first arrived she 'was scared to walk through the streets because there were men selling drugs.' She didn't think that the attitude of the local community towards newly arrived Somalis was a good one. Now it is 'one hundred percent better' and the young people of the area are doing better. She feels a greater number of young people now have jobs or are going to university.

With the support of the Liverpool 8 Law Centre, her mother was able to join the family. Thinking about her early life Fatima said 'when I came here I cried every day. I missed my country but now I never go back very much. Maybe every three years. My children tell me they are English people, they were born here.'

Hawo, Asha, Isir, Halima, Mariam, Fatima,
Lodge Lane Women's Somali Group

Stories from the Merseyside Somali Community Association

Tony Wailey visited the Somali Community Association on Granby Street on a number of occasions and interviewed, Abdilahi Awad, Abdi Hashi Guleid, Mohammed Farah, Mohammed Yussuf and Abokar Jama Ogleh, all connected to sea going in Liverpool. This is their story.

Abdilahi's Story
Abdilahi Awad

People often forget that there was no official Somali language until 1972, the divisions of north and south of the country have always been there. Most of the old Somali seamen came from the northern territory of what was British Somaliland. Since the late 19th Century, the ports of Cardiff and Liverpool in particular have always contained Somali seamen. Their numbers grew after the Second World War and grew again after the civil war in Somalia, when many of the older seamen sponsored families escaping from the conflict.

I never knew my father. He died when I was 3 months old. I was constantly searching for my father's photo but someone had destroyed it. I chased up all references to him and found his discharge books and the ships he had sailed in. I found a photograph there. I used merchant navy records and other websites. When my uncle died over 12 years ago, a small box of his papers were found in a shop in the town he came from. There was a list of all the seamen who lived in the town but also all the seamen there from my father's shipping days.

I have a brother who was born in the 1930's who worked for many years as a welder in Cammell Lairds. He is 12 years older than me and knew our seaman father well. You will find many interesting stories of the Somali seamen, where they came and went, where they settled, had families and the areas they came from.

Many Yemeni seamen came out of Aden to settle in Liverpool; there is a great tradition of Somali and Yemeni settlement in Liverpool from the late 19th Century to the Second World War, that is how new generations came to the city and again after the civil war.

My story is similar to the book about Somalia and Yemen, *Black Mamba Boy* by Nadifa Mohamed, about a boy in Aden who has to go back to Somalia and yet cannot rest until he discovers where his father's (who has been absent from his life) remains are. This leads to a great journey, across Djibouti, Eritrea, Sudan, Egypt and across the sea to Britain and freedom. Nadifa interviewed many of the older Somali seamen and got their stories to produce this great work.

Mohammed's Story
Mohammed Farah

I first came to the seaman's street of Upper Hill Street. Somalis, Jamaicans, West Africans, all the seamen used to live on those streets. I came to Liverpool 8 in 1964. I arrived from Birkenhead with a cargo of grain from Canada. I had no permanent address until Upper Hill Street - I stayed here then after the first time I arrived. North Hill Street is exactly the same as Granby in the old days. I stayed and shipped out of here ever since.

I stayed my first night in Atlantic House and then I walked up Hardman Street to Catharine Street and onto Upper Parliament Street and that is where I met all the people.

My family joined me in 1975 with 3 children and we had another 3 children in Cairns Street. I bought my house there at no 1 Cairns Street.

I used to go back to Somalia every couple of years. The children were small, one was seven, one was three and one was just eight months and we had another 3 in Liverpool. I stopped sailing in 1980. The kids were small and my wife couldn't speak the language. I left the sea after 29 years.

I sailed all over the world with Harrison, Blue Star, Shaw Saville, Burns Line, Tramp ships to Canada, Australia and China. I often go to the Pier head and I look over at Mann Island and I see all the glass buildings and think they say there is no money.

Voyages were very hard before 1972, you signed for 2 year contracts. Voyages were hard for everyone, you could be away 2 years on the charter, there was a lot of chartering then. We were sailors, most of us Somalis were sailors, AB's.[1]

The Union was good in the 1970s and became very strong - Jim Slater was good and conditions changed for the better. We were all in the NUS it was just a shame that as conditions improved for everyone all the jobs started to go. Many Somali seamen have died in Liverpool.

There were lots of cafés on Upper Hill and North Hill Streets. There was a Somali café on Great Church Street in the 1950's. Somalis have moved up from the docks, they just used to walk up from the Queen's Dock. There was a Somali hostel on Upper Stanhope Street, just like the club on Upper Parliament Street. They used to call Beaconsfield Street, Somali Street because Somali families lived at no 7 and no 9.

All my family are in Liverpool, I have 12 grandchildren who come and see me. The seamen's mission used to give us money but now they don't. We are means tested, they said we were too rich. (He laughs).

In the old coal burners most of the Somalis were firemen. When the ships turned to oil, the Somalis started to come on the deck. It was a very hard job for the stokers.

The old firemen used to buy camels when they got some money, they were known for it. The Somalis always used to go back to the country, the Somali seamen came mainly from the north, where the people are nomads. They buy a camel and live in the villages. Old firemen sometimes had five or ten camels, they were regarded as very rich.

We never saw a thousand pounds, never. My wages were 16 pounds a month as a Junior Ordinary Seaman until I got my tickets and then my wages doubled. There's a couple more fellers we can bring here, older Somalis if

---

[1] Abbreviation for Able Bodied Seaman

you want to talk, fellers who have been here since the second war. They can tell some stories.

We often go back to Somalia, but the kids don't want to go back any more. They don't 'get' the old ways and some of them have lost the language, they are Scousers. Who says the Muslim people are not integrated. Is Norman Tebbit still alive? (He laughs). He wanted to test us on integration.

We stay two or three months when we go back, we go with our wives but we are all getting old, sometimes my wife goes by herself or sometimes I go by myself or sometimes with my old ship mate here (he turns to Mohammed Yussuf).

Abdi's Story
Abdi Hashi Guleid

Our major port was Berbera on the Red Sea. The union changed everything after the war. I jumped ship in Hull, worked for a time at Immingham docks for six years, had a family and then came to Liverpool where all Somali seamen are. Many Somali seamen jumped ship here and then went back to sea from Liverpool. When they went back to Somalia they would not go to the towns but would return to the bush and the desert. They did not stay in the towns. I always have my breakfast here in the community restaurant.

Mohammed's Story

Mohammed Yussuf

I sailed all around the world. I lived in Cardiff and I lived in Liverpool. I left the sea in 1973 after 25 years. We were shipmates once Mohammed and me, but we are old friends and all our children remain in the community. I left the sea and went to Warrington, worked in a factory and bought a house there and all my children were born there but they always came back to Liverpool for the community. I come to Liverpool all the time and spend time in the Centre. My wife came over here in the early 1970's – all my children, six of them were born here. They have all moved to Liverpool now and live and work here. They are all in their 40s and have their own families, except one who is back in Somalia, a maths graduate, he could not get a job here.

Abokar's Story
Abokar Jama Ogleh

I sailed on Greek ships for five years - ships registered in Athens; Piraeus was the port we sailed from between 1969 -1974. I joined many chartered tramp ships there. Then I started sailing from Liverpool in 1975. I was working on auxiliary ships for the Royal Navy. I sailed on British ships all over the world and on many lines until 1990, most of it with Blue Star and Shaw Saville chartered ships and tankers and of course the navy, but I was always merchant navy. I gave up after twenty years because there were no more ships. General cargo is finished because of the containers, even the tanker trade, which you could always find work in, is declining with the growth of the super tankers.

Group Summary

Liverpool was always a very segregated city, now it is changed, you see black people all over the place, in Anfield and in Kensington. Many more people from the Yemen and Somalia now live in Liverpool 8. Many of the old seamen sponsored the new families – family reunion. Islam is much stronger in the new community – the constant wars in the Muslim countries have changed many people. Since 2001, the security checking of the Muslim people does not help. If you go to America and you are Muslim, they can check you for up to ten hours. Security measures like these do not help.

Young Muslims are not as free as we were. Even across the Arab states, everything is checked, you go Dubai or Oman or Jordan; the same restrictions apply. Those restrictions worked in attitudes of many of the young people.

There is more indirect racism now in the USA and Britain. Britain is more hypocritical. I sailed with an Irish Catholic boy, he told me he could not go buy a house in certain areas of the city; they knew him and knew which areas he had to live in. There is still the same tarnish, if you are not William Johnston from West Africa, you are Mohammed Ali Hassan; names, let alone skin colour, still work against you.

We are completely integrated but sometimes it does not feel so. We are happy with our history in this city. We are Somali and we are British and we are Scousers (laughter again).

Abdilahi Awad, Mohammed Farah, Abdi Hashi Guleid, Mohammed Yussuf, Abokar Chama Ogles,
Merseyside Somali Community Association

Hazel's Poem

Hazel is a member of the Granby 4 Streets Community Land Trust; proud to live in The Granby Triangle which is sharp and pointed like some of its residents.

A Rant About The Bins

Hazel Tilley

This is a rant about bins and how other people always seem to know the best way for us to live.

So, houses are knocked down,
because someone who's never walked down Granby Street
Knows how to improve our area and the best way for us to live,
And people are moved, because the shops are closing down
And the area's neglected.

And the other people, the ones who know the best way for us to live,
smell money.
So, they neglect the history of each brick and slate and skirting board,
Of each life spent in each house.
They neglect the little lives of little people who don't know the best way to live,

They neglect how each house, and life and family, how each street came together.
And the people who know the best way for us to live
remove the lead from the roofs of the houses they emptied,

To stop it being stripped and stolen and sold by us,
Who don't know the best way for us to live?
So that we can't buy drink and drugs or heating or food
or a present for those we love,
Who also don't know the best way for us to live?
And money and ideas and promises change hands
between
The people who know the best way for us to live and the
people they consult
Because, they too, know the best way for us to live.
And what of us? The people who don't know the best
way for us to live.
We remain unseen and neglected like the houses.
And rain penetrates the houses and the floorboards weep.
And the people who know the best way for us to live
Are shocked by our audacity and stubbornness
when we refuse to change the way we live
Even though it might not be the best way for us to live.

When we refuse to leave our homes, and agree with their
consultants
When we ignore the wisdom of the people who know the
best way for us to live
And we make something of the neglect of shops and
houses and people
And build gardens in our streets and make space for a
market and dreams
We can do this, because we don't know the best way for
us to live.
And other people visit us, they come to see the people
who don't know the best way to live
And they write about us and film us and paint us and
make art in our streets

And they congratulate us on our stubbornness and audacity.

And the plants and the dreams grow, in a messy, organic way, and our stubbornness and audacity grow too.

And the rain penetrates the houses and the floorboards weep.

And the people who know the best way for us to live, smell money

So they pretend to listen and tell us, when they need publicity, how great we are,

Even though we don't know the best way for us to live

And they promise 'to keep us together' when they buy our houses from us

And we refuse to change the way we live.

And the politicians change, and the people who know the best way for us to live run out of money

And break their promises and feel it's a shame that we had audacity and stubbornness

And they just don't know how to help us and they shake their heads and walk away

And the plants grow and our dreams shine

And the rain penetrates the houses and the floorboards weep.

And us, the people who don't know the best way for us to live, cheered

And we carried on being stubborn and audacious and we gathered together

And think we might smell money now, being a small part of the Big Sodding Society.

But the people who know the best way for us to live,

Fill our nostrils with bureaucracy and virtual paper

And tell us 'we are on your side' and smile and say 'we

share your values'
And whisper aside, but you can't share our money.
But they know the best way for us to live,
So they give away the houses they let rot and scatter a crumb or two towards us,
The people who don't know the best way for us to live.

Listen up now, you don't know the best way for us to live
And you don't share our values.
You, who think you know the best way for us to live,
Who squabble over the bones of power and pose for the smell of money
Who can't imagine the way we want to live
And whose values are such that they can't be shared by our values
You don't know the best way for us to live
You moved people who didn't want to move
You tried to close us up and sweep us into corners
You saw a 'big picture' and a 'whole solution'
And where you saw messy, we experienced variety and home and life
And when you couldn't shut us down, you left us
The people who don't know the best way for us to live
With the rain penetrating our roofs and our floorboards weeping.
You, with your talk of the World in one City
Break up the heart of it and leave its history to crumble
And we don't go away and bit by bit we reclaim our streets.

You don't help, you can't think small enough to know what to do with people and their messy, organic, piecemeal lives, with dreams and value and who have

found a way to live.
And in a messy and piecemeal way the rain stops penetrating the houses
And the weeping floorboards are comforted
And people move in and streets light up.

And, sometimes, on Wednesday, the bin men drive round.
And nobody gave much thought to where we keep the bins
Not even you, the lots and lots of you,
who know the best way for us to live.
And what of the bins I hear you say.
Well that's for another rant for another day.

Seafarers of Port Sudan

Zena Mekki

I suppose this is about karma and how it comes in many different forms. My dad, was Ali Beshir Mekki. I suppose like most children you take your parents as you find them and you expect the same from any other adult. Pops, as we called him, was just that. He was the centre of our universe, the centre of our family and above all else we were taught respect by him and Mop. They worked hard from early morning till late at night; before our shop opened and way after it closed.

When I was very young I remember lots of people from all over the world coming to visit us. I never really understood who they were and many of them brought us presents. Much later in life - in my 20s probably - I learned that these were seamen or newly emigrated people from different places. Many of them continued to visit our family for years. I remember some settled in Liverpool, some moved on to other cities and some remained at sea. They continued bringing gifts. We called them Uncle because they were so much a part of our family.

What I didn't realise was that my father and mother were instrumental in helping them settle and find homes here. They continued like this for most of their lives. They would never shout about it. They were humble. None of us children knew about it until many, many years later and never from them. The stories slowly seeped into our awareness from different people, children of those people, children's children of those people and that is just in Liverpool.

This story happened thousands of miles away in

Egypt. It involved my brothers Jaffa and Beshir, my sister Sakina, Serean Benoni and a friend of Besh's. They planned this huge trip that would last at least a month, visiting my Aunt Sakina's family in Egypt and then on to Sudan to visit the family where my Pops was born.

He was one of 19 children, only 5 were girls. He left home at 15 to go to sea and send money back to his family. He supported the British war effort on one of many of the merchant ships providing supplies during the war. One of these ships was torpedoed and he had to swim in shark ridden waters to survive.

He was later diagnosed with diabetes and not able to continue as a seaman. He settled in Liverpool in the 40s and began to build a life. As a hard worker my dad took his savings and began a business and from this he bought property. He did this because of the colour-bar that excluded many of his former shipmates from renting or having a place to bed down while their ships were in the port. I remember as a very small child sometimes when the ships were in, Pops would take us on board. The gangplanks were like huge wooden mountains to climb. Pops would buy produce for the shop that couldn't be bought elsewhere, like okra and molokia, and egusi, things that would be for African, Arab and Malaysian families, so as well as providing a welcome place to stay, he also provided the comfort of home foods. And this is where the story of karma becomes evident...

About 20 years ago, after planning and saving for the long trip. Jaffa travelled with the group and arrived in Egypt only to find that his baggage had not arrived with him. The group then went to the flat, which one of our more wealthy cousins in Sudan owned. The following day they returned to the airport and Jaffa's backpack was there but after walking back through Cairo to the flat, Jaffa found he had been pick-pocketed. His passport and the money he had saved for so long had gone, every penny of it!

My elder brother, Ali was able to send some money to him but when he tried to get his passport replaced at the British Embassy, the Egyptian staff would not believe that he was a British citizen. He also tried to report the theft to the police and they would not believe that our cousin who is very dark skinned, was family, and tried to prevent him entering the station to advocate and translate for Jaffa. It later transpired that the police were corrupt and were trying to procure money from Jaffa. It took four weeks for him to get a passport and only after going to the embassy every day did he eventually get to speak with a British member of staff there.

Once they were able to travel, they booked tickets on a ship bound for Saudi Arabia then Port Sudan. This would be a lot cheaper than the flight they had originally planned, but it would take two days sail. They boarded the ship and settled in amongst the other passengers, most of whom were setting off on Haj to Mecca. Despite the misfortunes Jaffa had, they talked of the time they had spent with our aunt Sakina and many of the 'off the track' places they had taken the group to. It had worked out well and they had enjoyed the trip so far...

At dinner-time they went for their evening meal only to find that the Sudanese ship would not accept either Egyptian or British currency. They had no food or water and were two days on board. Jaffa asked to speak with the captain to try and negotiate a way of feeding the group. He has a way with people. While talking, the captain asked where they were from and on hearing that they were from Liverpool, told them of his student days there. His next question was 'Do you know of Ali Beshir?'

When Jaffa told him they were his children he changed from an official to a brother. He said '79 Granby St' in such a gleeful manner. The captain told them of how our father had taken him under his wing as a young man and he called him Uncle Ali. He told them he had lodged in Jermyn Street and if he wanted anything, my Pops would point him in the right direction or provide it. From that point the group spent the two days eating with the captain, being given a tour of the ship and even being allowed to steer with the Captain's guidance. Jaffa described it as feeling like royalty.

He said the name of our father is known around the world and his good name from 79 Granby St and his legacy still lives on.

There are many stories similar to this that we as a family have discovered and how much Mop and Pops have been quiet, humble members of our community, yet have impacted in many positive ways on so many people's lives.

Sunday

Helen Thompson-Kwofie

I was born in 1952 and lived in Upper Stanhope Street. Before that, my family came from High Park Street, and my mum's mum was from Everton. Her family, half Irish and half Welsh, were called the Blair's. She married Mr Walker, a black man, so her family disowned her and we lost touch with that side of the family. My dad's mum was from Scotty Road. She was half Irish and half Scottish, too. His dad was a seaman from the Ibo tribe of Nigeria.

When I was a young girl I used to go to Granby Street mostly on a Sunday. I was only allowed to go with my brother and sister while we waited for our Sunday roast to be ready. Granby was the place to be! We'd just hang around for a bit, talking and having a laugh, leaning on the cars that the big lads left parked up. There would be music playing… It was really lively!

You'd try to get home early so that you could go back out when your dinner was finished. But whether you got home early or not, you'd have to wait 15 minutes for your meal to digest before they let you out again. By that time you'd only have about half an hour left, because it was school the next morning.

Sometimes you'd go to Granby for the shops with your mum. I mean, most of the time we didn't have to leave our estate because there was everything in the shops round here, but my mum used to go the watch repair shop, and sometimes it was useful that the halal butchers on Granby was open on a Sunday too.

In those days you had the woman coming round with the toffee apples – the brown ones, not those red ones they have now. These were the best toffee apples you ever tasted and the apple inside was dead juicy! I'd like to see more shops back on Granby.

Singer Seaman

Beverley Williams

I was an only child and did not have a big family although mum was the eldest of 11, she left home to marry dad, as she was white British and her family were unaccepting of her having a black boyfriend/husband, who was also a seaman. She moved to Toxteth where her and dad lived in a flat in Kingsley Rd until they married and moved to Mulgrave St L8 when I was born. We moved to Skelmersdale when dad got a job, I was aged 5. We returned to Toxteth as all their friends were in L8 and dad experienced racism on a regular basis in Skelmersdale. They bought their house with dad's redundancy in Cawdor Street, off Granby, which was later CPO'd by the council for a 'regeneration' of the area. They moved to Coltart Rd off Kingsley Rd where they both lived happily until they passed away, still retaining connections with friends who had been dispersed from Granby Street.

My dad, Bill, was lead singer of a group originally named Delroy Stephens & His Comando's, later to be named The Caribbeans who played at Palm Cove and other local clubs at the time. The members consisted of: Roy Steven; trumpet, Bill Davis; bongos/lead singer, Owen Stevens (Roy's brother); tenor sax, Leslie Stevens; alto sax, Wayne Armstrong; double bass, Sammy Loggins; drums, Desmond Henry, drums. It was one of the most popular (if not THE most popular) clubs amongst West Indians and was open every night.

Different Mixes
Abdulla Nagi (Adam),

Father, Grandfather and Great Grandfather

I came to live in the Granby area in 1984 shortly after the 1981 riots. I remember there was a Co-op opposite Danny's and Mohsen's shop is the one on the corner of Granby/Selborne Street (called Nabil's).

When I used to get a taxi, the driver would inform me that he was only willing to take me as far as Princes Road and refused to go into Granby. I would get off at Princes Road and walk through into Granby.

There was Macro cash and carry on the corner of Beaconsfield/Granby Street owned by Ahmed Sultan. I bought the Macro from Ahmed and began to settle in the area.

Shops and houses were cheap, even in Lodge Lane there was a shop, including upstairs accommodation, which sold for three and a half thousand and these days they ask for thirty to fifty thousand pounds just for the business lease.

While Granby had its community unity, there was crime; for example, people used to get robbed when they used to go to the Post Office, and even when I had the shop, a young man snatched the handbag of a female customer.

They used to tell me that back in the 60s and 70s Granby was so lively that music played into the early hours was normal. People socialised till dawn like it was day.

The area had a mix vibe of crime and safety. People used to come from all over Liverpool to shop in Granby.

There were shops and services which served your needs.

Now it looks like there isn't any land to build businesses, it's become endless rows of houses by developers.

Kojak

Abdul Qader Alkhanshali (aka- Kojak),

Father and Grandfather

Although I didn't actually reside in Granby, I was a regular to the area, it was full of shops, and there were Yemeni shop keepers from different parts of Yemen. I remember the fish mongers and the grocery shops.

People might have seen us as a threat when we made our way outside Granby in big groups, but that was for protection from the skinheads around the top of Lodge Lane and Lawrence Road. The police would drive around and find any excuse to grab you and throw you in the back of the Land Rover - they were extremely racist.

I used to live in Entwistle Heights but the comfort zone was Granby. We all used to make an effort to dress well; we used to go and socialise in Stanley House on Upper Parliament Street. There used to be a 'ladies house' on Selborne Street.

I can still remember the afro on my head, ironed shirt, flares and smart jackets. But when we went out I used to wear silk pants, long black jacket with a red handkerchief sticking out of my top jacket pocket. You never went out on your own. We would join the other black young men and were spoilt for choice as to where to socialise. There were lots of social clubs in the area.

I got the name 'Kojak' because after an incident I was hurt and had to go to hospital where I needed stitches in my head, that meant the doctors had to shave the area where they needed to stitch and from then on I was given the nickname 'Kojak'. Sometimes I drive down Granby Street and look around but it's not the same.

Derelict

Anonymous

Derelict – it doesn't serve the community
There used to be facilities for every nationality
Many who once cared have now changed their philosophy
A social breakdown – dereliction of duty

The Village

Carol Bennett

My Granby Story started in 1991 when I came to work in Toxteth. I had applied for a job at the Caribbean Centre and was due to attend an interview at Amberley Street. My husband and I drove past the night before to see where the Caribbean Centre was, but for the life of me couldn't find Amberley Street. After circling the block, along the avenue, Mulgrave Street and down Upper Parliament Street several times, to prevent getting arrested for kerb crawling, I decided to stop at the post office/store on the Berkley Estate. As I approached the counter with the Liverpool A-Z book in my hand a lady in the queue turned around and asked if she could help me. I told her what I was looking for and she told me that she was the centre cleaner and she would show me where it was. Toxteth is like that, it's like a small village where everyone is friendly and willing to help one another. She got into our car without worrying about her own personal safety or that I would kidnap her and showed me where the centre was. It was the building on the corner of Mulgrave Street that we had passed four times already but she told me that the car park entrance is all that remains of Amberley Street. I got the job and became the administrator and I worked at the Caribbean Centre for 12 years. Granby Street is very dear to me. It was vibrant and colourful and a fun, safe place for children to learn.

In 1991 Toxteth wasn't a safe place for children to play in the street and parents kept an eye on their own and one another's children. The streets of Toxteth were the first in Liverpool to have riot vehicles patrolling the streets on a daily basis and multiple police vehicles respond to 999 calls in the area. Toxteth was also the only area where there was a staffed 'cop shop' in the middle of the community – admittedly with CCTV cameras on the street watching what was going on. People were frisked on the street in unwarranted Stop & Search pull ups by passing police cars. I witnessed a family of five in their church clothes one Sunday pulled up on the street because the dad was carrying a stereo ghetto blaster. He was asked to produce the receipt! Toxteth was the first community in the UK with a drive through bank. It was also the area which hosted Princess Diana in 1995 when she came to meet families who had been given new build homes under a 20 year old regeneration plan developed in 1981.

The youth club became a charity in 1993 with a committee made up of local people, mostly parents. It moved every few years so children in other parts of the area could benefit, operating in St Johns Youth & Community Centre on Park Road, The YMCA in Mount Pleasant, Toxteth Sports Centre, Granby Cop Shop, St Bernard's Church and the Neighbourhood Office on Kelvin Grove.

When we were in St Bernard's Church Hall on Kingsley Road we had a funder came to visit us at the youth club one weeknight. We had submitted an application to the Morgan Foundation and Steve Morgan himself (of Redrow Housing fame) came to meet the children and young people. He didn't send his secretary, or his grant officer, he came himself. He came in a chauffeur driven car but he came because he wanted to see the area. He wanted to see the project first hand. It wasn't that he didn't believe us (that we were delivering what we said we were delivering) it was that he himself originally came from Toxteth. He made a big contribution to the club over three years, which helped us to develop sustainability, which was much needed at the time.

Toxteth is still like a village, as I often meet mums on the street, at community meetings and in the supermarket and they tell me about their children being parents now, if they are working and what they are doing now. Some are at University, some are married and one went to jail. I also meet grownups who were the beneficiaries – they recognise me and think that I will remember them despite me last seeing them when they were 10 or 15 or 19. Adults, both male and female, will come up to me to say that they still remember going to Ingleton, or Playaway, or Derbyshire. But the best one I remember is two girls behind me in a queue one Christmas telling me how I took them to Barn Farm and one said her Nan still has the peacock feathers the farmer gave to her on the day we came home. Occasionally I will be standing at a bus stop and a car will pull over and the person behind the wheel is someone who did driving lessons at the club. They won't take no for an answer and insist on driving me to my destination.

I have bumped into the same people on social occasions, at weddings and community engagement events and it shouldn't really surprise me after all Toxteth is just like a village where everyone knows everyone else. When I was made redundant from Victim Support one of the old boys told his mum, who in turn told the committee at the Somali Women's Group and they offered me a job as administrator before I had even served my notice period at Victim Support. I now work there and I am the centre's activity co-ordinator, developing new leisure & recreation projects and fundraising – very much doing the same as I always did in 'the Village' of Toxteth.

I know lots of interesting people who all have one thing in common; even if they don't live in Toxteth their connection is that they want to be there and they love working there. I keep getting drawn back and I am sure I will remain here until I retire.

Honest Streets

Lubna Alawi

I first came to live in Granby in 1992. I barely spoke a few words in English. I lived in Beaconsfield Street, then I moved to 36 Cairns Street where I had my eldest Wasam, and then moved again to number 37 Cairns Street where Reham was born. I remember those years very well and have many great memories.

From what I can remember, all the houses in Cairns Street were lived in, apart from possibly two houses. I was neighbours with Gina and Kevin, one of their sons was around the same age as my son Wasam and I used to look after them both at the same time, feeding them and changing their nappies. It was a relaxed neighbourhood. We were like an extended family regardless of race or religion; we shared time, food and outings. Our children played together including the other children that lived in the street.

When I first arrived in Granby I would smile at the neighbours, as I wasn't confident in trying to speak English. Then I began learning a few words. I would greet people by saying 'hi' or 'good morning', followed by a brief conversation from them, in which I would respond by agreeing to what they were saying, which was normally about the weather and what a nice day it is.

My English has improved a lot and now I can hold a good conversation and took on the British cultural habit of complaining how wet, cold or miserable the weather is!

One day, while living in Cairns Street, an elderly man

and woman, along with their grown up son knocked on the door and explained that for many years they had lived in the house I was living in and they asked if they could come in and reminisce. I welcomed them. They were remembering where they used to have their furniture and how it was; they took photographs of themselves in the house and the back yard, after their trip down memory lane, they thanked me and left.

I can recall a time when living in Cairns Street, myself and a friend decided to go out together and from the morning till eleven o'clock at night we went socialising, shopping and it wasn't until our return that my friend realised that she had forgotten her bunch of keys still in the door! They say Granby is a bad area. I don't think so!

We would look forward to the Caribbean carnival, Halloween but mainly bonfire night. Our whole families would get involved; we would collect wood from all over Granby and pile it up around the wasteland by Javy's international food shop.

On bonfire night, many people would join us in gathering around the bonfire; we would all wrap ourselves in thick coats, boots, hats, scarves and prepare our corn on the cob, tea and coffee for our social mingling until very late at night. You were most likely to see people you knew or hadn't seen for a while on that night.

When needing anything from each of our neighbours we would either knock on each other's door or send the children. Every morning I would open my curtains and look across the road to my neighbour's house or watch the children play in the street.

Due to a reshuffle I was moved to Seaport Street and have been here for fifteen years. Now I open my curtains and see a brick wall and wooden garage gates. Despite that, I would never move to another area. I feel I would not belong anywhere else. It is safe and comfortable here in Granby.

Due to new houses being built, there has been the compulsory removal of shops, for example Javy's international food shop where we were accustomed to him and bumped into locals for a chat while doing our shopping.

While it's good to have more houses built due to the extra demand of people wanting to move into the area, we are losing more shops and have less land.

I would love Granby Street to have a mini mall with a post office, cafe, and social area, clothes shop and advice centre.

Childhood Shops

Arwa Baggash

My name is Arwa and I am 39 years old. I have written about my lovely memory of Granby and I'd like to share this story.

I can remember as a young child coming to the Methodist Centre when it was a nursery, my mum used to take me and my brother. We cut through the alley way and reached the nursery to play half a day, it seemed a long time but it was good. I played in front of my house with my brothers and the pavement and road looked so big and spaces to me looked like football pitches, you could ride bikes, played with hoola hoops, football and sometimes if the weather was nice we had a picnic by the front house. My mum would do some laundry washing and, because there was no child care at that time, we would sit on top of the counter eating chips, and they were the best chips ever.

Weekend's granddad would take us to the Mosque, we would sit on a ledge and watch everyone doing their prayers.

There were plenty of shops in Granby. We had a cash and carry, chemist, video shop, post office and you'd have your local butchers.

There was one time mum used to tell me to go to the shop and get cornflakes and my dad didn't have any in the shop. I'd go to Seba's shop and ask her, so she'd give me the item. One day dad went to Seba's shop to buy shoe polish and he got a surprise to find out he had a large bill to pay, he wasn't impressed with us. We learned from that mistake.

When I look back at this I wish it could be like this now for another generation to see.

Hard Girl

Ms Hannah Ali, Mother of five

My Mother and Father arrived from Yemen to Granby in 1976 and soon after they bought their Grocery shop. We were a community of Yemenis, black British, mixed race, white, hardly any Asians or Chinese.

I was born in Granby and went to Granby School then St Mary's, which is now Bellerive School. I was a tomboy in my younger days, I used to played football with the boys. I would put my track suit on and hoody and play Kerbie. In fact I think I don't even remember what the girls looked like!

There was life in Granby. I remember Grants off-licence, Mohamed's newsagents, Halima's newsagent, Danny's (who is still there) Norma too. Ken the barber, who had four shops. I used to go to the chippy and go and eat them while sitting on top of the washing machine in the laundrette. Rex the watch shop and the chandlers were there too.

Bonfire night was amazing. We would have a huge pyramid of wood and anything that burnt in preparation for the social night. We would be ecstatic as we prepared to warm up in our thick clothes. There was one of the locals in charge of the halal burgers.

While the bonfire was burning and the music was blasting. I would sell tea for £1 to my Dad's friends who had gathered at the back of the shop playing cards.

Religion wasn't practised as much, it was more cultural. The Yemeni women didn't used to wear the hijabs like today. Apart from my Mother; she was the only one who did wear it from ages ago.

My Father was a real hard knock; they tried to rob him, threaten him, but nothing put him off from living there, he was up for a challenge. There used to be groups of black young men around the street and they knew I was easy to wind up so one would nudge the other and say 'Oi, Paki!' As young as I was, I would flip and give loads of abuse back. Plus I was confident that I had back up if needed.

I would not think of the consequences I'd just react. When I'd argue with the boys we'd end up in a fight, and I mean a proper fight. My father would come and just watch, he always said, if you are going to take it on, take it to the end or don't take it at all.

I remember the 80's riots and my father grounded me for protection, but I still got out. If there ever was a situation where the police were called, it would be over one hour before they came.

One side of me was the boisterous kid, another was the girl who went to the Mosque every Friday, the holy month of Ramadan and Arabic School at Paddington Comprehensive, (now known as Archbishop Blanch) Monday – Friday from 5pm till 8:30pm…

I don't think there should be any more houses built in Granby Street itself but we need more shops. I'd like to see a chemist and other community led shops.

I miss the Granby life so much. I currently live in Upper Warwick Street, but waiting in anticipation to be offered a property in Granby.

Nineties Diva

Nicola Duzant-Hayden

I was born the winter of 1981, January 13th in Oxford St hospital. My mother was an artist who loved music and fashion. We lived in a small flat not too far from town, based in Percy St. The area I lived in (Toxteth, L8) was poverty-stricken. But we were surrounded by creatives, people who understood the nature of art and music. A place with broken down buildings cursed by a political riot, which in a funny way gave the area a sense of character.

My childhood was filled with the green smell of Princes & Sefton Parks, my favourite places in the summer. Always lively but peaceful at the best of times (a great thinking place), although there was always somewhere to go, I would always look forward to visiting my friends in Beaconsfield St, where the residents there would have a street party for all the children.

As time went by, we then moved to a small flat at the bottom of Grove Park (Lodge Lane). My friends there were cool but were very different characters from my friends at Beaconsfield (Granby St). As much as in reality I was only living ten minutes down the road, I felt like Lodge Lane and Granby St were two different worlds. In my world, my perception of the people around me was that we loved music – there was nothing better. Our lives revolved around it. As a teen, sneaking to clubs and live parties could not be helped. We were drawn to the sounds, hungry for Hip Hop, Soul, Jungle, Bashment and R&B. Lying in bed at night listening to a local Pirate radio called Shaka FM.

Growing up, my mother (RIP), who I loved dearly, always encouraged me to do as many activities as possible. From the age of three I had always been in the entertainment industry, like others around me. Showing our own local talent, the underground sound was the sound we projected. Carnival was one of the happiest times of year. Family, friends, music and good Caribbean food. 48 hours filled with dancing from tent to tent. The field covered with a sea of Caribbean colours from people in carnival costume.

The 90's era was a time of hot summers, girls dressing like TLC and weekends at afterhours spots called The Blues. With other events popping up known as Phat Skillz, Players Ball, and then Bounce, The Blues was the spot to go to once the event was over. This was held in the basement of a food cafe/shop called Spices. The focal centre point many would say of Granby St. Throughout the years, great moments come and they go. We remember the parties and great music created. A time that once felt like it stood still is now waiting to re-emerge. The hidden talent and culture of L8 is waiting beneath the surface.

This is my story.

A Story of the Blues

Paula

1977 and we are going mad learning every lyric from the X-Ray Spex album in my bedroom, on an estate where all the houses look the same and nobody looks like me. Occasionally I agree to come out of the room to make the too long, two-bus journey with my Nan to visit her father on Enid Street. The second bus puts us off on Princes Road and we walk the rest of the way. Granby Street is just one of the mythical type places that feature in my Nan's stories, usually about something that happened 'in the war'.

1987 and I've come from London for the weekend to visit a friend who's moved to Princes Avenue and I fall in love. Not with anyone, but with the forgotten grandeur and the street signs painted red green and gold. I notice there are people that look like me. Lots of them. It feels like there is something special about the place, but I can't really grasp it and I don't try explaining it to my friend, because it sounds nuts, but somehow the air seems different here, drenched with memory and possibility. My friend talks about the 'front line' and a graduate now, I've read about Granby Street in sociology books. Still I don't realise my proximity to the place nor the fun that awaits. On the Euston bound train, with Eric B & Rakim on the Walkman, I decide that one day the view from my living room window will be that Victorian boulevard and like them, I ain't joking.

1997 and I'm rocking in front of a giant speaker, oblivious to all except the baseline that pounds through my body. Cloaked in total darkness there's no feeling like it. The lighting of a spliff reveals for a moment the face of a smoker who also has surrendered to the heavy, heavy dub sound. Eyes may meet through the blue grey haze but a slight nod speaks volumes and is the only communication required, unless you need to ask someone for a Rizla of course. This is the Frontline where they play only reggae. I come here a lot. My friends, they're mainly from Aigburth, think it's dangerous so mostly I come alone. There aren't many places you can comfortably do that as a woman, but there is nowhere I feel safer. Saying that though, a few weeks ago I did find a machete under my foot. When I handed it over to the DJ he said 'what did you bring that in here for'.

In the mood for something more lively, I nip across the road to Spices. The music's more R&B with a bit of other stuff thrown in. From the stairs into the basement I hear the DJ shout 'hold ya lighters up' and beneath the sea of tiny flames, I see that the place is rammed. I recognise some mums from the school and the girls from the flat downstairs in their pyjamas for a dance before bed. I learnt to love Jungle down here. At first I couldn't feel the seemingly disjointed super-fast beat and didn't know how to move to it, but in the darkness no one is watching and you just go with it. They call it Drum and Bass now it's become more popular and they play it in some clubs in town but it was played here first. Walking home now up Granby, no need for a cab. Tired but energised at the same time. I cross over Princes Road to my flat on the other side of the avenue where the view from my bedroom window is the boulevard.

The Inspector

Carl Williams AKA Inspector

The first sound system I ever came into contact with was Gibby's at Mr John's on Princes Ave. It was in my mid-teens, and me and Nze used to go there and we started getting into mixing. We were influenced by the local African sound system, and they used to let me have a go at mixing.

We got into playing at the Gladray, Jamaica House and the blues. Blues or shebeens used to pop up all over the area in those days and they always needed a sound system.

Me and Val Reid went halves and bought a little Amstrad sound system with a record player, tape-to-tape and mic input. We used to sit off listening to sound tapes and Daniels would get on the mic and start chattin'. We had a little bar as an incentive for man to get on the mic, but sometimes we didn't practise for long before we got wasted. We used to practise in my mate's flat above Rex's watch repair shop.

After that, we went to some funding bodies, but they couldn't, or wouldn't, help us, so we eventually saved up our own money and bought a state-of-the-art 15,000 Watt sound with hard vinyl scoop bins. It pumped out 'nuff bass!

Our first real jobs as teens were at Toxteth Carnival. The organisers, World Promotions, would give us the keys to a van, ask which marquee we wanted, then give us a cheque and free promotional t-shirts. We were introduced to big sound man like Macka B, Baron Turbo Charge and Stereo Dan.

122

We called ourselves One-a-Penny Sound System and we were the first North sound to ever win the Gold Cup, which we did three times in a row. After that we played all round the community and used to take coach-loads of people with us to other cities.

After the carnival stopped, we used to mostly play at the blues on Granby, and out on the streets on sunny days. We did that for 20 years. Spices, Trash 'n' ready – we played all over!

When Granby quietened down, it felt like something was missing.

History Sounds

Gary Daniels

My Great-Great Uncle was William Gordon Masters [2], also known as Gordon Stretton. He used to walk from Vauxhall in to Lancashire and was in the Lancashire Lads Dancing Troupe, at the same time as Charlie Chaplin. His musical skills took him around the world, and he was one of the jazz pioneers of the 1920's.

I didn't know all this when I first started getting into music. I only found out later on. When I was young, I lived in Tennyson Walk and went to Windsor Street School. The only time we used to cross Granby back then was going between the Unity Centre off Lodge Lane and the Meth on Beaconsfield. But as I got older, Granby Street became my cultural playground. There was music, endless conversation and Jamaican food. When the poolroom opened, then we really had somewhere to hang out. Then there was the record shop with the arcade games and fruit machines - you could even buy leather hats and pouches there.

After a while, me and the boys started getting into the sound systems. I used to go to Inspector's and get on the mic and start toasting. When we got our own system, I learned to 'make the machine work', which is what we called sound engineering. Looking back, I know now it must have been in the blood. We could play music all day, whether it was at dances, the carnival, or just on the street on a sunny day.

Granby was a focal point for the community.

---

[2] Billy Masters sailed to Paris after the First World War where he founded one of the largest Jazz orchestras on the Continent. He would later introduce Jazz into Latin America where he fused it with the rhythms of the Tango. From his base in Buenos Aires, he remained many years on the Argentine. (editor's note)

124

Big and Small World (1)

Amira, aged 10

It is nice coming here because I like playing with my friends. I also like it here because I like the shops to buy some sweets and crisps with my friends.

And many more years ago there used to be lots of shops but now we don't have many but we are trying to get more shops in Granby Street.

I also like it in Granby Street because it has a club named 'The Methodist' and it has been here since the 1940's and it was modernised in the 1960's. It looks after all the young children and supports them and we do lots of stuff in the Methodist such as painting, pool, football, netball, studio and sometimes poems. And we used to do dance, drama and singing. And it was very much fun (and I think we might do it again). And my Nan loves to come here but she is tired when she has to walk here to Granby Street.

Big and Small World (2)

Rahem, aged 10

It's fun because we do poems here. I like poems because my Uncle likes to write poems. My Uncle has a job of writing poems. My Uncle's name is Ramkes.

My Uncle has been writing poems of when he was a little kid and of the past life in Granby.

I live in Lodge Lane near Granby. My Mum drives me to the Meth, we do fun things like painting and football.

I like poems because it's fun to make words go together. It's nice here in the Meth. I like doing painting and football and also the studio (it's a recording studio and we make CD's). In the summer holiday me and my Cousin Amira have been with our Mums and we went to Sakoon on Lodge Lane. My Uncle is the owner of a shop called Sprinkles.

The End

Curtis's Poem

Curtis is a performance poet, rapper, actor, presenter, musician, beatboxer, workshop leader and author of *Children's History of Liverpool*.

To Granby for a Chili
Curtis Watt

Everyone used to talk about Granby Street –
mostly about crime.
A place where gangsters and dealers would meet,
most of the time.

I was from the other side.
My mum said to stay away.
But I walked over – well, cautiously snuck –
one memorable summer's day.

In those days I was quite a thief.
I know now I should have known better,
when I stole some fruit from the grocer's
that turned out to be a chili pepper.

See, I'd never seen a raw chili before,
so that's why I'll never forget it.
I took a bite and then rubbed my eyes,
and instantly knew I'd regret it.

I saw no gangs or drugs that day,
just a few kids and people out shopping.
But still this was alien territory,
so we all walked straight on without stopping.

Then, by my mid-teens, my estate was knocked down
and I got to know Granby quite well.
A thriving centre, a place to hang round,
just years before it fell.

The Dancer

Linda Freeman

I remember happiness, and the sometimes uncertainty I had living on Cawdor Street, off Granby. I saw the beauty and potential of all who lived here, unfortunately I also witnessed the demise of the community we shared.

Decisions were made about Granby going back some time which affected Granby and started the decline of a vibrant settled community. I believe decisions made by the Council as early as the 60's started Granby's decline.

They started on 'Husky', Huskisson Street moving us out of houses and demolishing streets to make way for a road. The road never happened leaving people in doubt. Then a move which closed the Princes Avenue entrance to Granby Street in the 70's. This stopped passing business made to the shops which affected local trades, affected profit margins.

Then in the 80's they put more bollards up and traffic calming measures to stop 'joy riders'. There was even talk about building a wall around Granby and its housing estate.

First it was containment then it moved to dispersal, homes were boarded up, people were CPO'd out of their homes, told to move on. Protests started and planning applications were approved. Houses started to empty. Boarded up, streets died.

We continued to live our lives despite the uncertainty, shopkeepers fought planning applications to CPO their businesses and won, but most had despaired of a successful outcome and were bought out for less than their value and trade projections. People fought for their homes after much hardship and heartache. To date positive moves are in progress, resident led, to rebuild the Community we had stolen from us.

I reminisce about Bonfire parties for the kids, where Darrel and the gang collected money to give the Community fantastic community displays and food cooked by the Mums with homemade toffee apples and baked yam and potatoes in the fire to boot.

We lived within many contradictions. We watched war zones drive refugees from across the world here, Vietnamese 'boat' people, Somali seamen who had fought in the Second World War, and as merchant seamen had done the dangerous Atlantic and Arctic runs. How they fought to have their families reunited with them when war hit Somalia, expanding our Somali families across the Community. Biafra's refugees in the 60s fleeing the Nigerian war, Chilean refugees had come in the 70s. Ugandans, Asians, white South Africans, white Zimbabweans, exiled ANC activists and then Kosovo refugees. People from the Congo, Iraq also arrived in stages in the 90s as war ravaged their safety. Many brought here by Westminster Council as they made cheap deals with property speculators to provide hostel accommodation on the cheap, without regard for the impact on services that were needed to support them or the quality of the hostels they were put in.

Our young people could not get housing, one bedroom flats became the domain of house seeking students as a 'better class option', nothing for the young unemployed or on those training courses, who couldn't afford the rent.

Some left for London. 'Giz A Job', whilst some fell afoul of the 'marching powder', whilst others never gave up.

We continued to build organisations around our needs. Determined to keep what was good in our Community alive. We were entrepreneurial, we built organisations and to fund them, we danced!! We danced in the Ibo, the Freetown, the Carousel, Jamaica House, the Gladray, Federal, Eureka, the 'Nige', the Caribbean Centre, we danced in the blues. I recall we danced for the Carnival, to raise funds for the independent candidate, the LBO[3], the Black Caucus and more, we danced for the miners' strike to feed them. We danced for the carnival and funds for the kids. We danced for the bonfire parties and to feed and clothe the refugees, we danced to raise funds for the ANC[4]. We danced for Black Sisters and the mentally ill at ease. We danced for the elders social events and MST;[5] through all the contradictions of the regeneration game when they moved our ward boundaries to marginalise us out. We still loved our Granby, warts and all, even those who have moved away see Granby as the heartland of L8. May we keep on dancing to make Granby great again.

---

[3] Liverpool Black Organisation
[4] African National Congress
[5] Merseyside Skills and Training

Congratulations to all those published in *Pitt Street to Granby*. Thank you for producing such quality writing and being generous enough to share their stories with us.

Writing on the Wall is a dynamic, Liverpool-based community organisation that celebrates writing in all its forms. We hold an annual festival and a series of year-round projects. We work with a broad and inclusive definition of writing that embraces literature, creative writing, journalism and nonfiction, poetry, song-writing, and storytelling. We work with local, national and international writers whose work provokes controversy and debate, and with all of Liverpool's communities to promote and celebrate individual and collective creativity. WoW creative writing projects support health, wellbeing and personal development.

If you have a story to tell, or would like to take part in, or work with WoW to develop a writing project, please get in touch – we'd love to hear from you.

Mike Morris and Madeline Heneghan, Co-Directors

info@writingonthewall.org.uk
www.writingonthewall.org.uk
0151 703 0020
@wowfest